Read what the professionals have to say
about Hidden Messages:

"As usual, Elizabeth Pantley offers a book that is respectful to parents, clear and readable, and absolutely helpful. Without judging or lecturing, this book helps parents give children the messages they really want them to receive."

—Kathy Lynn, President
Parenting Today

"Through both laughter and tears, in each story you will see yourself, your family, or simply someone you know. Once you have composed yourself, you can read the follow-up to the story to learn both the hidden message and changes that you can make. Elizabeth Pantley is making it a habit to write both entertaining and helpful books in a style uniquely her own. Read this book for sheer enjoyment, but also read it for the lessons learned."

—Jill Lassaline, Creator and Editor
ParentsWorld.com

"Elizabeth has done it again! While reading *Hidden Messages*, I found myself saying . . . 'Oh, that sounds like us.' It truly hit home and gave me the answers to questions I've been asking myself for years. It's refreshing to finally find an author whose life is so parallel to the common family. *Hidden Messages* has made me see the light!"

—Janice Boyles, Publisher
Choosing Home, the newsletter for
at-home/work-at-home moms

"This book has already made a difference in my parenting! I saw too much of myself in these parenting pitfalls. Elizabeth Pantley's advice is important and will help parents treat their children in a more considerate and effective way."

—Betsy Gartrell-Judd
Managing Editor
InteractiveParent.com

"If I didn't know any better, I would swear that Elizabeth Pantley was hiding in my house while writing this wonderfully eye-opening book. So much of what's written here hit home that I found myself often nodding in agreement while poring through its pages. On several occasions I found myself in tears, saying, 'Yes, I have done that!' Hats off to Mrs. Pantley for once again bringing us a wonderful resource to be referred to time and again."

—Amanda Formaro, Creator
The Family Corner.com

"*Hidden Messages* is the Rosetta stone of parenting, helping parents to 'crack the code' and shed a ray of light into the darkness of parent-child miscommunications. Elizabeth has proved to possess great insight into the problems we all face as parents. The format is light and easy-to-read in the spirit of her previous successful works, *Kid Cooperation* and *Perfect Parenting*. She has forged another tool to help us to better understand the people we love. We highly recommend her books."

—Joe Spataro, M.D., and
Sue Spataro, R.N., B.S.N.
Parent Educators and Creators of
Family Education and Online
Health Communities

"Another winner by Elizabeth Pantley! This book reminds us that kids are people too, and what we say to them and about them makes a big difference in their lives. It points out commonly overlooked negative messages that we send our children despite our best intentions. But even more, it shows us concrete ways to use positive language and productive actions to direct our children toward more successful futures."

—Jill Whalen, Editor
Parentsroom website

"Once again, Elizabeth Pantley's talent as a parent and a parenting educator shines. Effective and kind communication is an essential parenting skill, and no other parenting book that I've read covers this topic so thoroughly and thoughtfully. Realistic situations, practical suggestions, and emotional impact make *Hidden Messages* a very important book for all parents."

—Keri Baker, Creator and Webmaster
Parentingweb.com

"*Hidden Messages* is quite a find! Here are easy-to-read yet provocative stories that encourage parents to look inward. Pantley explains how well-meant words can convey unintended—and harmful—messages to kids, then offers sensible suggestions for avoiding such parenting pitfalls. The result: kids who cooperate cheerfully, accept responsibility, and feel good about themselves."

—Tamara Eberlein, Author
*When You're Expecting Twins,
Triplets, or Quads; Whining;* and
*Sleep: How to Teach Your Child to
Sleep Like a Baby*

"*Hidden Messages* is an insightful new look at parenting. Through stories of real families, this book explores the implications of things parents do and don't do for their children in the course of everyday life. Don't miss the empowering, supportive advice found here to help children feel loved and become healthy, happy, capable adults."

—Shelley Butler and Deb Kratz,
Authors
The Field Guide to Parenting

"We are what we eat is evident to people who care about their physical health. Of equal concern should be the verbal diet that we feed our children. *Hidden Messages* admonishes us to give our children the positive, thoughtful verbal nutrition that is so often lacking. A must-read for all parents."

—Ray and Lynne Heinrich
Ontario Stepfamily Association,
Canada

hidden messages

what our words and actions are *really* telling our children

ELIZABETH PANTLEY

CB

CONTEMPORARY BOOKS

Library of Congress Cataloging-in-Publication Data

Pantley, Elizabeth.
    Hidden messages : what our words and actions are really telling our children /
Elizabeth Pantley.
       p.   cm.
    Includes index.
    ISBN 0-8092-9770-1
    1. Child rearing.   2. Parent and child.   3. Communication in the family.
I. Title.
HQ769.P266   2000
619'.1—dc21

                                                        00-26128
                                                            CIP

Cover design by Jennifer Locke
Cover photograph copyright © www.comstock.com
Interior design by Precision Graphics

Published by Contemporary Books
A division of NTC/Contemporary Publishing Group, Inc.
4255 West Touhy Avenue, Lincolnwood (Chicago), Illinois 60712-1975 U.S.A.
Copyright © 2001 by Better Beginnings, Inc.
Printed in the United States of America
International Standard Book Number: 0-8092-9770-1
    3 4 5 6 7 8 9 10   DSH/DSH   0 1 0 9 8 7 6 5

This book is dedicated to my children:

Angela Elizabeth
My firstborn, my angel.
Now nearly a teenager,
and as delightful, respectful, and joyful
as you have always been.
You're a special young woman, and
you make me very proud.

Vanessa Marie
A face created from happiness, a heart that brings peace,
laughter that lights up a room.
You bring me great joy and fill my life with a special soft love.
You are a precious gift to me
and to this world.

David Robert
Your desire to protect me and take care of me
and others in our family,
your delightful sense of humor,
and your passion to make this world a better place
make you an extraordinary young man.
You have a very special place in my heart.

Coleton Alexander
My delightful baby.
You have brought a whole new world of wonder
to our beautiful family.
Thank you for giving my heart
one more precious child
to love.

Note

This book is designed to provide parents and caregivers with a variety of ideas and suggestions. It is sold with the understanding that the publisher and the author are not rendering psychological or professional services. This material is presented without any warranty or guarantee of any kind, express or implied. It is not possible to cover every eventuality in any situation, and if further guidance is necessary, the reader should seek professional advice. This book is not a substitute for competent professional counseling.

Some of the stories in this book are absolutely true. Some are compilations of anecdotes that parents have shared with the author over her years as a parent educator. (We'll let you guess which is which!) With the exception of references to the author and her family, all of the names and identifying features have been changed.

Contents

Foreword

A child's self-image is affected—for better or worse—by the messages he or she receives from parents and caregivers. As a pediatrician and father of eight, I have the privilege of knowing many families. Their approaches to child rearing are as different as the very children they raise, but the vast majority of parents have one thing in common: they want only the best for their kids. These parents try, on a daily basis, to do the right things and to make good parenting decisions. Many of these parents, however, actually make faulty decisions based on, or in spite of, those good intentions. These mistakes are sometimes insignificant, but more often, they have enough impact to cause problems that can affect the futures of both the child and the entire family.

So, why do good, well-intentioned parents make bad choices? Sometimes it's a matter of bad advice; sometimes love for a child makes parents vulnerable to unhelpful advice; sometimes it's a set of incorrect assumptions; sometimes it's a lack of knowledge. But the most tragically common reason is that *they are simply not aware of the full impact that their words and actions have*. At best, the evolution of a good parent is marked by moments of revelation, in which the parent is shocked to see the potential long-term effects of a mistake—and is able to change course quickly. At worst, the discovery is made much too late, the wrong path already taken.

Elizabeth Pantley's new book, *Hidden Messages*, is the wake-up call every parent needs, a consciousness-raising journey through the small moments of parenthood. Each chapter uses warmth, compassion, and humor to draw the reader into a common, everyday scene in the parent-child relationship. The reader will laugh, cry, or gasp in recognition over and over again—until the story reveals the unintentional but clear message that is quietly and unknowingly being sent from parent to child. It is then sure to bring a moment of revelation.

The story alone may have enough impact to startle the reader into making crucial changes. But *Hidden Messages* doesn't stop there. It goes beyond the story to dissect the errant message, discuss its source, and lay out its possible and logical consequences to the child's well-being. And, most important, it offers specific suggestions for revising those hidden messages so they communicate more positive, growth-enhancing lessons.

This unique book is sure to gently tweak the consciences of even the best parents, inspire them to raise their children in a more conscious and sensitive manner—and tug at their heartstrings as a reminder to give constructive messages to their children.

—William Sears, M.D.

A Note from Author Elizabeth Pantley

Dr. Sears is my parenting hero. His books came to my aid when I was a nervous and inexperienced new mother twelve years ago. His wisdom and knowledge helped me learn what it really means to be a parent, and his gentle insight showed me how to do the job in the most loving and successful way. I am deeply honored that he finds my books so helpful to parents that he is willing to write the foreword for each one. My perception is that most parents know Dr. Sears—and those who don't, should.

Dr. Sears is one of America's most acclaimed and respected pediatricians, an associate professor at the University of California

School of Medicine. He is host of America Online's "Parent Soup" and is pediatric and parenting expert for the "Parentime" on-line service. He and his wife, Martha Sears, R.N., are the parents of eight children and the grandparents of four. They appear frequently on national television, are extensively quoted in the media, and are the authors or collaborators of twenty-four parenting books, all of which I enthusiastically recommend. A partial list of Dr. Sears's work includes *The Family Nutrition Book, The Discipline Book, The A.D.D. Book, The Baby Book*, and *Nighttime Parenting*.

Acknowledgments

I am very grateful for the support of the many people who have made this book possible, and I extend my sincere appreciation to:

Judith McCarthy, at Contemporary Books. An editor and mother who recognized that the material in this book would be of value to parents, and whose guidance helped create the finished product.

Meredith Bernstein, of Meredith Bernstein Literary Agency, New York. An agent whose honesty and experience continue to help me fashion new and helpful parenting books.

Dr. William Sears. For teaching me to parent from my heart. The greatest amount of appreciation for his work and guidance would surely come from my children, Angela, Vanessa, David, and Coleton.

Vanessa Sands. My special friend whose brilliant editing helped make this book an emotional journey for parents and caregivers.

Kimmy, Tyler, Rachel, and Zachary Sands. Thank you for lending me your mommy and for providing her with daily love and inspiration.

Shelley Butler. For her insight, her honesty, and her willingness to share her knowledge on the "technical" aspects of parenting education.

Keri Baker, Janice Boyles, Janet Chan, Bobbi Conner, Tamara Eberlein, Amanda Formaro, Betsy Gartrell-Judd, Ray and Lynne Heinrich, Deb Kratz, Jill Lassaline, Kathy Lynn, Joe and Sue Spataro, Jill Whalen. All of these colleagues, when asked to review and endorse this book, not only did so graciously but also provided positive, enthusiastic, and encouraging feedback.

Dolores Feldman. My angel of a mother. Thank you for always being there to listen to my writing drafts with the support and unwavering confidence that only a mother could provide.

Robert Pantley. My best friend, my love, my rock, my adviser. Thank you for eighteen years of support, wisdom, love, and joy. I never knew a honeymoon could last so long. And it just keeps getting better.

Introduction

None of us is born knowing how to be a parent, any more than we're born knowing how to drive a car. When we decide to learn how to drive, however, we take lessons, read the manual, and practice—a lot—before we take to the road. But when we become parents, we're forced to hop into the driver's seat with no experience and—for many of our number—very little knowledge or skill. We're driving recklessly at best, blindly at worst. Either way, we can endanger lives if we're not careful. It's important that we take the job of parenting seriously—seriously enough not to follow the easy road, seriously enough to consciously examine how we parent our children, seriously enough to change when necessary. A thoughtful, organized, calm approach—in which we slow down enough to identify our mistakes, and make adjustments to correct them—will keep us all from careening uncontrollably off the shoulder.

How? First, it's meaningful to admit that you don't know it all when it comes to raising children. No one does. The scope and magnitude of the job are immense, and every child is unique. But wisely acknowledging the need for more information opens new avenues to success.

If only the intricacies of child rearing could be detailed in a paragraph or two in a nice, concise manual! Still, as a mother of four, I am acutely aware that each child would require a unique edition. Every person—whether child or adult—differs from the next; add to that the myriad ways in which parent and child interact, and you have a situation that can't be tidily predicted. So, all you can do is gather the information available, keep the ideas that seem promising, and adapt that advice to what you know of your child's singular makeup. This is your responsibility as a parent. Countless books, tapes, classes, and support groups offer innumerable strategies to parents willing to search them out. I hope, through this book, to encourage you to invest the considerable time it takes to learn the many skills necessary to raise capable, responsible, polite, and enjoyable people. You are on the right road—after all, you care enough to read a parenting book.

Hidden Messages is a very *different* kind of parenting book. It explores the hidden messages that good parents inadvertently send their children. It examines the seemingly healthy everyday interactions between parents and children to find the surprising problems lurking beneath. The stories themselves are parables of a sort, gleaned from the hundreds of accounts that parents in my groups have relayed to me through the years. Each story seeks to teach a gentle lesson by shifting perspectives—from that of the parent to that of the child. After each episode, I identify the hidden message and then discuss the problem's impact on both parent and child. Each segment concludes with suggestions for specific changes you can make to help you best employ the lesson illustrated.

As with so many situations in life, half the battle is discovering the mistake; the other half is fixing it—and becoming aware of the potential for error can sometimes prevent it altogether.

Nobody has all the answers; nobody's traveled to all the places that parenting can take us. But with a little personal examination, persistence, and commitment, you can find enough parenting tools to ensure the confidence you need to teach your children the rules of the road, and to direct them toward their own successful futures. I sincerely hope that the panorama that follows will help you achieve that goal.

How to Use This Book

A Few Ideas and One Important Question

"When you sell a man a book, you don't sell him twelve ounces of paper and ink and glue—you sell him a whole new life." This quote, by Christopher Morley, clearly states the real purpose of a book like this one. If it can entertain you along the way, so much the better—but it's not my main purpose in sharing these stories with you. I hope to provide some useful insight into the surprising hidden messages that you may be sending your children along with clear, specific suggestions to change those messages into something more positive and nurturing.

As I was writing this book, I passed along a few sections to friends. Many of these friends then volunteered some unique ways in which they applied the lessons to their own lives—some ways they'd made the lessons work for their particular families. I'd like to share three of their ideas with you.

Theresa's Idea

"I love a good mystery. My favorite pastime is to curl up with a book and guess my way through the twisting plot of the story. When Elizabeth offered to let me read a bit of her new book, I eagerly accepted. The title and concept intrigued me. As soon as I read through the first story, I knew how I'd approach the rest of them to derive the most benefit from them.

"I read each story with a keen eye to the details, but I always stopped reading before Elizabeth revealed what hidden message the parent in the story was sending. I went about my day's activities, and I thought about the story, trying to uncover the clandestine message. I occasionally went back to the story to check on a detail or two. After a time, I guessed what the moral of the story was. With my guess in mind, I continued reading to discover what the hidden message really was.

"With some of the stories, I had been able to decipher the message before it was explained. Then I'd move on through Elizabeth's suggestions, learning how to avoid (or repair) any parenting mistakes.

"Some of the stories were a real puzzle to me and opened my eyes to new ideas. When I read 'Baby Love,' I discovered a timely and poignant lesson for my own life.

"In a few of the stories, I uncovered a hidden message that was uniquely my own. A different lesson from the one in the book, but a lesson nonetheless, that taught me something I was very glad to know.

"Regardless of the outcome of my search in each story, I found this book to be a starting place for new discoveries in my personal journey through life as a parent."

Naomi's Idea

"I'm an introspective person, given to reading the types of books that require contemplation and digestion. I took home Elizabeth's manuscript pages with an eagerness to find their meaning in *my* life. I found quite a few stories that described me to a tee. As an avid reader, I know that much of the profound and life-changing material that I read becomes a vague memory as time passes. I was determined not to let that happen to the wisdom I found here.

"When Elizabeth offered me a choice of stories, I happened to choose the section that addressed my biggest parenting mistake. I laughed at the accuracy of the description. Even now, thinking of the title makes me chuckle: "Hamburger." The parenting mistakes described in all of these stories could be made by *anyone*. I saw my sister in those pages as well as a friend or two. But in this particular story I recognized myself so closely that I had to shake my head in amazement.

"I wrote out notes of the most important points. I took one key word from these notes and copied it onto a stack of index cards (I will let you discover the word on your own!). I taped these cards onto the front of the dishwasher, the laundry room door, the coffee table, and anywhere else where my 'mistake' most often occurred. I found that this simple reminder helped me modify my behavior. I was so proud of myself for using what I had learned to make an important change in my life—a change that would encourage my children to grow into more capable human beings."

John's Idea

"Elizabeth gave me a few excerpts from this book, which I took with me on vacation with my daughters, Roxanne and Liza. The girls were playing in the water as I relaxed on a lounge chair, reading. Rox, the oldest of my two at eleven years old, climbed out of the water and wandered over to me. 'Hey, Dad, what are you reading?'

"'It's part of a new book Elizabeth Pantley is writing.'

"She paused for a moment, struggling to recall who Elizabeth is. When she remembered, she asked, 'Is it for parents?'

"When I told her it was, she asked if she could read it, too. Since the story I had just finished was 'Daddy, Play with Me,' about a father's relationship with his daughter—and since I was currently showering her with quality time on this vacation—I acquiesced.

"Thus began a discussion that lasted, off and on, the entire afternoon. Rox and I read each story together and talked about the family in each one as if we knew its members. She eagerly shared her perspective with me about the parent in each story.

"The hapless father in 'The Baseball Star' rated an angry and enthusiastic 'zero' on the Rox Scale of Parenting. I've coached Rox in soccer for many years, so I saw an opportunity to delve deeper into my relationship with my little-girl-turning-young-woman. Gathering all my courage, I asked, 'How would you rate *me* in this area?'

"After a moment of thought—an eternity of a moment during which I watched her face strain with the effort of diplomacy—she pronounced me an '8.' She explained, 'When you first coached me, you kind of expected me to do too much. But in the last two years, you're really doing much better.'

"Story by story, we talked, she rated, we laughed, we hugged. Elizabeth's book opened dialogue between my daughter and me on many topics.

"Now, I'm smart enough to know that sometimes, in the effort to save her poor dad's feelings, she wasn't as honest in her rating as she could have been. And, I know that a child's perspective on her parents changes daily, depending on the hundred small things that make one day different from the next. But, I also know, with all the certainty in this father's heart, that this one afternoon of sharing was more than just a fun deviation from the norm, more than a day she and I might remember fondly. It was a day—and a book—that brought our relationship to a new level of understanding."

One Important Question

These three parents found a way to apply the information they read toward their own personal growth; they let the lessons help them create positive changes in the way they raise their children. They allowed this book to give them "a whole new life." Can this book give *you* a whole new life? That's really up to you. As you sit down in a comfy chair and begin reading these pages, I hope you'll take a minute to ask yourself one important question: "What's the best way for me to use these lessons to improve the lives of my children and my relationship with them?"

I

Messages of
Responsibility
and Independence

Hamburger

Curt, a bright sixteen-year-old, was bursting with excitement over his newly earned driver's license. His mother, seeing an opportunity for him to exercise his helpful tendencies, as well as his newfound freedom, asked him to go to the grocery store to get some hamburger for dinner. The look on his face was jubilant! His mom had never trusted him with even such a minor task, preferring to do it herself so there was no room for error.

He grabbed the car keys and made a mad dash for the garage before she could change her mind. She went to the kitchen to begin dinner preparations. She sliced the tomatoes, defrosted some buns. By the time she'd finished her preparations and set the table, she began to worry. More time passed—and still more. Where was Curt?

Just as she was considering a trip of her own to find him, Curt trudged through the door—without hamburger. "Where's the meat?" she asked.

He shrugged his shoulders. "They don't sell hamburger at our grocery store, Mom."

"Of course they do, Curt!" she exclaimed, wondering what her son was up to. But he sighed loudly and persisted, frustrated that his mother didn't get it.

"I went down every aisle twice, Mom, and they do *not* sell hamburger!"

Exasperated, she asked Curt to get back in the car, and she climbed in beside him. On the way back to the store, she muttered under her breath, "It's just like I've always known it was around here. If I want something done right, I have to do it myself." Once at the store, she marched over to the meat counter, Curt dragging just behind. She pointed dramatically and announced triumphantly, "There!"

She was stunned when her son, looking puzzled—a tall beacon in a sea of cellophane-packed ground meat—said, in the sincerest of voices, "I don't see any hamburger . . ."

It took a few seconds for her to make the connection. Her son—her driver's-license-toting, beard-growing, college-bound son—had never been allowed, or never been asked, to help with grocery shopping! Nor had he ever prepared a meal! The truth was that he couldn't recognize raw hamburger if she threw it at his head! Well, that head was currently shaking back and forth in amazement. "Wow," he said, "I've never seen it like that before."

When the fog cleared, other thoughts crept into her head: He'd never done a load of laundry! He'd never balanced a checkbook! He'd never changed a flat! He'd never sewn on a button, or mended a tear in his pants! He'd never even packed his own lunch! Since she'd always done all that for him, he'd never had the opportunity to do it for himself—and now her son, who was rapidly approaching full adulthood, had no idea how to perform any of these common rituals. She, with all the best intentions mixed with a bit of all-too-human impatience, had unknowingly failed to prepare her son for his foray into the real world. She was a good mother—*too* good.

The Hidden Message

"Don't you worry about any of these tasks. I'll do them for you. I'll *always* be there to do them for you. You're not very capable, and you'd never catch on, anyway, even if I did try to show you."

Think About It

Sometimes, raising responsible kids isn't so much about what we do, but about what we *don't*. By being "too good" of a parent, we rob our children of opportunities that help them develop tools for success in adult life—tools that can't be bought or given, but must be forged by experience. Every task we complete for our children is a task not done *by* our children.

I can imagine you now shaking your head at this page in protest, asking a valid question: "But my *job* is to take care of my children! Aren't these tasks a part of my *job*?" Read this answer slowly and carefully: *No.*

Your job is to raise responsible, capable young people who eventually leave your home to build independent, productive lives; your job is to help them develop the skills necessary to do just that. So, you should feel good about teaching and transferring some of your household duties to your children, knowing that this is an essential gift that you're giving them.

This is a process that should begin early and continue at a regular pace. Introducing important life skills to your kids when they turn eighteen isn't feasible and might just be impossible. For one, teenagers are busy; they are eager to get on with life and have little patience to learn mundane skills such as loading the dishwasher. For another, they've already developed habits that are hard to break. So, it behooves us to bring our babies into childhood with a constant eye toward what we're doing for them and weigh it against what they could be doing for themselves.

Having said that, I maintain that it's perfectly acceptable to *choose* to cater to your child at times. If your son is sick, of course, you shouldn't tell him to get out of bed and make his own chicken soup. If he is unable to complete a chore on his own—due to his age or abilities—it's an act of mercy to help him out. If you're fixing yourself a bowl of cereal, and your daughter is busy studying for a test, it's a nice gesture to pour her one too.

Consideration is a character trait every bit as essential as independence. The difference in these cases is that you're *offering*— your child isn't *expecting*. But do remember that the ultimate kindness in this vein is insisting that children help themselves at times and being clear about why.

Changes You Can Make

Begin by learning one useful word, to be uttered to yourself whenever you catch yourself doing for children something they should learn to do for themselves: "Don't."

This is one of the few times in parenting that you can be proud of the things you *don't* do. Next time you see that crusty cereal bowl, hum your mantra—"Doooonnnnn't"—and refrain from taking it to the sink. Instead, call your child, point to the bowl, and ask him politely to take care of it. When you see those clothes lying on the floor just outside the shower door, stop yourself—"Doooonnnnn't"—and ask your child to put them in the hamper. Don't pick up those crumpled-up snack wrappers left on the kitchen counter—"Doooonnnnn't." Request that your child give them a proper burial. Resist the temptation to move the morning along by packing your kid's lunch. "Doooonnnnn't." Instead, call her over to the counter and guide her through the lunch-making process.

These lessons needn't be dreary. For example, next time you're about to put in a load of laundry, don't simply trudge off to the laundry room—"Doooonnnnn't." As you pass your child, who is reclined on the sofa while watching TV, ask him to turn off the tube and join you for a quick laundry lesson. You both might take pleasure from the time you spend together, talking among the whites and the darks, enjoying a few moments of conversation as you teach another valuable life skill.

Yes, I know. You'll have to go though this drill again and again . . . But eventually, one bright day, you'll realize that some learning has taken place. (And just maybe your child will have caught on, too.) As if by magic, your child will have taken care of that cereal bowl without a word from you—and you can celebrate the fact that he's moved one step closer to being responsible for himself. And as a bonus, you'll have moved one step further away from frustration.

Of course, this approach calls for common sense. You can't expect a three-year-old to cook his own dinner, or a five-year-old to mow the lawn. Start with simple, age-appropriate responsibilities, and add to these as your child becomes more mature and capable. The beauty of gifting your child with the skills of responsibility and independence is that each skill is a building block upon which many others are balanced. First your child learns to count the spoons and fetch the napkins; then he learns to set the table; next he learns to fill his own plate with food; after that, he learns how to make the salad; and before you know it, he has the skills to prepare an entire meal.

My three older children—at the ripe old ages of eight, ten, and twelve—have the skills necessary to do exactly that. On several occasions, they have been given the privilege of planning and preparing a meal. The three of them discuss a menu plan and create a shopping list. Then Mom, Dad, or Grandma takes them to the grocery store, and the three kids do their shopping (as the adult in charge sips coffee at the front deli counter). They bring their groceries home and prepare the meal. It is absolutely delightful to listen as the three of them converse and discuss the details of the preparation: "Do you think these pieces are too big?" "How long do you cook beans?" "Do you think this is enough cheese?" The meals are very creative, usually colorful, and even tasty. In addition to knowing that they have learned important life skills, the glow on their faces as they bask in the success of their endeavor makes it all worthwhile.

So, how do you get to this point? If your little one is younger than six, consider yourself in the "training stage." This is a time when learning occurs and habits form. I know: it's so much easier to pick up your child's toys than to go through the labor-intensive process that "letting your child do it himself" really is. It does take more time and energy to "let" your child pick up his toys, tie his shoes, and pour his juice, as the "help" you need to give is often more complicated than if you had done it yourself. In the long run, however, you'll save yourself a virtual lifetime of catering to a child who never had the opportunity to assume these responsibilities at a young age. Such a child will see you as his personal valet and will resist giving up such a luxury. Wouldn't you?

Plus, taking the time and expending the patience to help a willing and enthusiastic three- or four-year-old learn to unload the dishwasher is a lot easier than trying to teach a busy, uninterested teenager, and then deal with the frustration when he doesn't keep up with it.

If your child is over six, every missed opportunity to teach a useful household task prolongs your child's dependence. Every single time you pick up a dirty sock, a used tissue, a crusty cereal bowl, or a misplaced toy—*every time you do this*— you teach your child to believe in the "cleanup fairy." This is not only frustrating for you but also difficult for your children when they move out of the house and discover that the "cleanup fairy" neglected to pack up and move with them.

This is one of those parenting tasks that are difficult for most of us. But the benefits are great. Perhaps the most wonderful payoff in allowing your child to master life through age-appropriate tasks and skills comes from the boost to his self-esteem. The more capable a child is, the more confident the child will become. With confidence, and a full repertoire of important life skills, comes a stronger, more positive self-image that will enable your child to take on whatever life imposes.

Mr. Fish Stick

In the course of every life are rites of passage, events that signal opportunity and growth. Sometimes they're heralded with great fanfare, but more often they're the seemingly insignificant goings-on of daily living. High drama or low, one characteristic marks them all: the growing person must rise to the challenge.

In first grade, my son David was called on to perform just such a rite: his first book report. With barely contained excitement, he explained that each student in the class was to choose an ocean animal and read about it, prepare a report, and create a visual prop. Library card in hand, he—newly appointed Big Man on Campus, given such a "mature" assignment—earnestly requested an immediate fact-finding trip.

While he spent more than an hour in the library pondering the many choices, I found myself delightfully pondering him. There he sat, a little boy among big books, looking so studious as he worked quietly and methodically. At long last, he made his decision. An already avid fan of sharks, he settled on the Great White Shark as his subject. I wanted to help him with his sizable stack of books as he maneuvered to the checkout desk, but his cool air of self-reliance stopped me in my tracks.

During the next few weeks, David became the resident expert on great white sharks. Tidbits of trivia sprinkled our daily conversations. "Do you know that some people call them the 'tigers of the sea' because they are so fierce?" (I didn't.) "Do you know it's hard to fight them because they are so strong?" (Like my book-toting little man?)

As the days wore on, David's growing pride in his success with such a lofty assignment shone in his eyes. He spent time every day reading and preparing material for his report. After much thought, David manufactured an ocean scene in a large shoebox as the required prop, scrounging though our craft supplies for needed materials. Although the only sand to be found was glittering purple and green from an old sandpainting kit, and clusters of painted macaroni had to do for coral, David pronounced the scene perfect. He glued on pebbles from the yard and covered the box in blue construction paper.

The crowning glory was, of course, The Great White Shark made from clay and from an afternoon of careful rolling and molding, rerolling and remolding. David's older sister, Vanessa, came into the kitchen as he was finishing. "What are you making?" she wanted to know. "It's for my project," David announced. "You guess what it is." Vanessa surveyed the shoebox ocean and pondered his clay figure. "Give me a clue," she said. David told her that it had to do with the ocean and his shark project. After a moment of thought, she asked, "Is it a fish stick?" I sucked in a deep breath, preparing to jump in and save the moment, when David threw back his head and laughed. "Yes!" he responded with glee, "Mr. Fish Stick, the Great White Shark!" I was delighted that my little researcher had a sense of humor, too.

At long last, the task was complete. David's six-year-old face glowed as he showed his finished assignment to everyone in the family. I was very proud of his finished work and happy to see that the shoebox creation did, somewhat, kind-of, look like an ocean scene. (Sort of.)

Well, at least, since I knew what it *was*, I could make out an ocean scene . . .

David and I were equally glad that parents were invited to attend school for their children's presentations. Out of pajamas and into the van in record time, he was so excited the next morning that we left for school early.

The students were to display their projects on their desks. David carefully arranged his artwork and report. A few minutes later, my eyebrows jumped to my hairline as I looked up to see a veritable parade of masterpieces: a marvelous papier-mâché creation of three dolphins jumping in unison above a colorful coral reef. A hand-sewn octopus sitting atop an array of rocks and seaweed. A large, intricately painted undersea display. Aside from the handful of projects made unique and charming by their journeywork imperfections, it was apparent that I now sat in the hallowed presence of divinely inspired talent—most of it in heads nearer the ceiling than the floor. And I noticed that those other less-than-perfect projects had creators hovering a lot more closely and proudly than did the more polished creations, with an eager narration that had only to be requested.

I overheard several of the other mothers talking. "I'm so thankful this is over!" (*I?*) "We've spent hours every night working on it." (*We?*) "I hope Brittany gets a good grade for all her effort." (*Hers?*) I could only hold my tongue and muse at the grade that would be missing from the report card—"Parent's effort and talent."

As David and I toured the room, I watched him for any signs of disappointment. I knew my worries were unfounded when he announced (of course, loudly enough for all to hear), "Brittany's mom sure made pretty dolphins." Ahhh. So it was obvious even to a child. It was obvious to the teacher as well, who directed the majority of her praise and comments to the children who had actually earned them. She chuckled merrily when David introduced her to "Mr. Fish Stick."

Once home, I reread the instruction sheet for the project. Sure enough, it said that "your child" was to write a report and "your child" was to create a visual prop. I found no invitation for "the parent" to create a project—and was sad for the children of those who did.

The Hidden Message

"Your work is not good enough. You are not capable, but I am. Let me do this for you, since I'll do it right. And besides, I can't be bothered to take the time and patience to show *you* how."

Think About It

Naturally, we want our children to succeed in school—so that they'll learn important skills, develop self-esteem, establish a good academic record, get accepted to college, graduate, and move into a fulfilling adult life. A primary measure of that success is the report card.

Without realizing what they're doing, and with the purest of intentions, many parents help their children achieve good grades in ways that actually sabotage their children's ultimate success. Consider Brittany, whose mom created a dazzling display of dolphins. She will most likely find her mother to be a full-time partner in much of her future schoolwork—that is, until Brittany reaches high school and Mom can no longer understand much of the work! Another possible scenario is that Brittany's mother perceived herself as too busy for open-ended library trips, messy painting sessions, and impromptu question-and-answer periods; instead, she opted to create a brilliant display herself and have the whole business done with. Either way, since Brittany is unlikely to develop the independence and confidence to achieve *on her own*, she may well find the complex demands of high school, college, and ultimately, adulthood beyond her ability to meet successfully. This, in turn, can trigger the very unhappiness on both parts that her mother had tried to prevent!

Changes You Can Make

Slowly, over time, rising to the challenges of homework and schoolwork helps develop a sense of personal responsibility, self-management, and resourcefulness. It's all part of a character-building process that begins with a clay shark in first grade, progresses through term papers in high school, and culminates in the crowning achievements of a satisfying life—be they in a high-powered career, humanitarian contributions, or excellence in parenthood. In helping our children toward all these accomplishments, our humble jobs as parents are to stand back, allow failure, and applaud success. Our hearts may ache with the stretching, as those of our children will, but we all know that an exercised muscle is a strong muscle.

The first important step for a parent to take? Simply turn over responsibility and ownership of homework and schoolwork to the child. This means that you and your child clearly understand that schoolwork is his "job" and one he must take seriously. This certainly doesn't mean you announce to your first grader that he's on his own while you take up your long-desired hobby of composing operas! While the parent should not be a full-time partner in homework, he or she should be coach, consultant, and cheerleader, overseeing schoolwork to help keep the child on target for work-in-progress and due dates. The parent should also make certain that a child has all the materials and supplies necessary, and help him to keep a daily schedule for homework. Also, avoid creating an environment of rewards or punishments to induce your child to complete his work. Instead, keep the focus on the learning process, show him where in his life he can use his new skills, try to inject humor where appropriate—and stand back and be amazed as the seed planted years ago blossoms into an independent and capable person.

Most important, we must remember that, however much we are tempted to succeed *for* our children, these rites of passage are solo voyages.

Fair Work for Fair Pay?

Andrea was eager to attend her parent support group this week. The topic at hand was one to which she had much to contribute— and from which, as it turned out, she and the other parents had much to learn.

As soon as greetings had been passed around, everyone had found a seat, and the group leader kicked off the round table, Andrea was ready to roll. "I've always been a strong believer in paying children for household chores," she stated. "After all, 'work for pay' will be the essence of their adult experience, so why not start them out that way as children?"

"That's how *we've* always approached it," agreed Rachel. "It's important for children to learn about responsibility; having them help around the house teaches that. I also think that paying them for this helps teach money-management skills."

Debbie added, "We've always used allowance with our kids as a measuring stick for performance. They know that when they do a good job, they can count on getting paid for it."

Brian nodded. "I've also found that withholding payment when the chore isn't done gives me some leverage! The kids usually get busy when I talk about keeping the week's chore money." The others laughed in agreement; it seemed that more than one parent had employed the leverage tactic.

Diane, who was seated in the back and whose shyness precluded her from contributing to all but the most compelling topics, wasn't laughing, though. Unlike most of the other parents there, she had older kids and had a different take on the issue. Shaking her head adamantly, she spoke. "You know what? If we'd had this discussion a few months ago, I would have agreed with all of you. But a few things have happened at our house recently that made me rethink my ideas." All eyes and ears turn to Diane. "I've always paid Trevor to do his chores, and it's always worked out just fine. But he just turned twelve—and he's been doing a lot more thinking, and he's coming up with some interesting observations." She sighed a parent-of-an-almost-teenager kind of sigh, then continued. "It started simply. I asked him to help me carry in the groceries, and do you know what he said?" The other parents shook their heads.

"He actually said, 'How much are you gonna give me if I do it?'" Quiet gasps ricocheted around the room.

Rachel's indignant response elicits a few chuckles: "Well, I'd have told him he'd be in big trouble if he *didn't* . . ."

Again, however, Diane did not laugh with the others. "It only gets worse! About a week later, Trevor was watching TV. I reminded him to take out the trash—it's his job, and it has been for years. Well, he looked up at me and, in a very innocent and polite voice, said, 'You know what, Mom? I have enough money this week. *You* can take it out.' He was serious, and I—well, I was speechless! When I finally recovered, I reminded him that it was his job. He said, 'But, Mom, you've always paid me to do it, and if I don't want the pay, I shouldn't have to do the job. Like last week when they called you into work on Saturday. I heard you tell Dad that it wasn't worth the money to give up your weekend, so you decided not to work. This is the same thing.'"

Paige, who had been quiet thus far, added her own story. "I'm so glad you brought this up, Diane. I've been sitting here wondering if I was the only one with this kind of experience. My oldest son came home a few weeks ago bursting with excitement because he got hired to work the summer at the car wash down the street. While we were talking about his new job, he announced that he'd much rather wash cars than do dishes and laundry. When I asked him what he meant, he said that his paycheck from the car wash would be enough money for the summer, and he wouldn't need his allowance. He just assumed that he was off the hook from all his chores! I realized then that, since I've always paid him to do his chores, his assumption made perfect sense!"

Andrea, grateful for the perspective that her parents group never failed to provide, went home intent on revamping her family's chore system. And she made a mental note to invite Diane and Paige out for coffee this week.

The Hidden Message

"You do your chores, you get your pay. If you don't want the money, you don't have to do the job."

Think About It

It's a common notion that children should be paid to do their household chores. Andrea voiced the most typical argument for this arrangement early on: that our world functions on a pay-for-work concept. This theory has a large gap, however; while adults do get paid for career-related work, they are not paid for the routine contributions to their own home and family life. They are not paid for the labor done out of love and consideration for those who share their home. When's the last time someone paid you for cooking your own meal, doing your own laundry, making your own bed, emptying your own trash? When's the last time your *family* paid you for doing these things for them?

Changes You Can Make

The vitality of any household depends on the performance of many tasks, day after day after day. These tasks should be divided among occupants, with a clear understanding that each person is part of a team, with the common goal of keeping the household clean, safe, and functional. Each team member needs to understand that he or she is on the same side as all the others, that there is no room or time for quibbling, and that the coaches (Mom and Dad) call the plays. Some jobs should be assigned on the basis of experience and ability: Mom or Dad must do the grocery shopping, since they can drive to the store and have the means to pay for the food. Mom or Dad pays the bills, since the children are not yet gainfully employed. Therefore, some jobs must be assigned to the children by default. The typical childhood chores of washing dishes, taking out trash, sweeping floors, and feeding pets are examples.

Over and above daily maintenance chores, it's perfectly acceptable to offer other jobs for pay. These should be considered "extras" and made available to kids who are ambitious and eager. These extra jobs can be house related, such as cleaning out the garage, watering plants, or washing the car, or they can be small conveniences for your business, such as stuffing envelopes, making copies, or filing.

Just as everyone in the family shares in the tasks necessary to keep the home running smoothly, everyone can also share in the family wealth. Allowances can and should be paid to children, with no chore strings attached and with the specific goal of teaching children how to manage money. But that's another story to be told . . . which leads us to the next story.

Gimme!

Winter's first snow promised more than a change in the weather: it heralded the fast approach of the holidays—and the annual gift-shopping ritual. Ken and Shelley figured that today was as good as any to hit the mall and get the deed done. Shelley stuck her head into the family room and called to the kids, "Ok, Nathan and Anna—time to go!"

As the four of them shuffled out to the car, Nathan was chattering about his friend's dad's new van. "Man, you should see it! The seats swivel, and there's even built-in headphones in the backseat for the radio!"

"Sounds nice," said Ken, squeezing in behind the wheel.

"So, Dad," Nathan continued, "why can't we have a neat van like that?"

"We'd love to," Shelley interjected, "but those vans are really expensive, and it's not something we can afford."

"We could always trade in a kid," Ken joked. Like most of his jokes, this one elicited a groan from the backseat.

In the front seat, Shelley was too busy to notice. She was reviewing their list of gift recipients, allotting price quotas for each. After a quick calculation, she asked Ken to stop by the bank. The kids watched as the ATM spat cash out of the slot as easily as Ken had put his card in. Nathan's voice popped up: "Hey, Dad! Why don't you just get more money from the machine and stop at the van dealership, too?" This time, it was the front seat occupants who groaned.

The first stop was to MegaToy City, a sprawling warehouse of material diversions—where even the carts were mega-size, presumably to encourage mega purchases. Nathan and Anna, as always, were awed and wooed by the colorful displays. One in particular provoked Anna to place her hand over her heart dramatically and sigh—a gesture Shelley recognized as her own. "Mom! Dad!" she breathed, "Here's the new Super City Electric Train Set that I saw on TV! And it's on *sale*! Can I get one, please?"

"Anna, we're supposed to be *gift* shopping today," her mother reasoned. "That means stuff for other people, not ourselves."

"Oh, but Mom," Anna moaned, "there's only three left on the shelf! We might never be able to get one!"

"No, honey," Shelley answered. "We're not buying it today."

But Anna remained rooted to the spot, nearly drooling at the glistening train set and taking inventory of the realistic city parts and pieces. "Mom. Pleeeeze? I won't ask for anything else for a whole year! I promise."

"Anna!" Ken's voice was firm. "You heard your mother. The answer is no. We have a lot to do today, so let's get busy." Anna's whole body drooped and seemed to be but an appendage of the lower lip she ceremoniously extended from her stormy face.

She followed her lip down another aisle, where Nathan's turn for pleading came next. "But, I've always wanted an Alien Mask with Adjustable Voice Changer!" Predictably, the previous scene repeated itself, and soon Nathan also wore The Lip.

Doing their best to ignore it all, Ken and Shelley continued agonizing over gift choices for cousins and friends. After more pouts from both children over various New, Improved, and Wonderful toys (Batteries Not Included), Dad finally relented and let each of them choose a new video from a wall that extended the entire width of the store.

The videos, however, didn't stop the whining that escalated with each new aisle they perused. The toy store became more and more of a punishment to the parents. Their cart was full of gifts, their limits for both cash outflow and patience reached. List or no list, Ken, Shelley, and The Lips got in line for the cashier.

Once their packages were paid for and the trunk loaded, Shelley suggested a lunch break. They stopped at the first fast-food restaurant that beckoned. They brought their order to the table, and faster than the parents could divvy up the little paper-wrapped parcels, Nathan reached across the table: splash! went his orange pop over his french fries . . . which then fell with a sodden plop to the floor. Neither Shelley nor Ken had the energy to complain. Luckily, a nearby employee graciously mopped up the mess and replaced the meal, gratis. Soon, the rest of the family was nearly finished. "I'm still hungry," Nathan announced, as if the world owed him a tummy-full of french fries but fell woefully short. "Well?" he added, annoyed that his thickheaded parents didn't get it. "Can I have some more fries?" With a second large bag of fries in hand, Nathan followed his family back into the car and out into the furiously shopping world.

At the end of a long afternoon, and with a fair amount of the list crossed off, Shelley wearily announced that shopping was done for the day. "I second the motion," Ken answered, his voice dripping with relief.

After they unloaded the car, Shelley wandered into the kitchen for dinner ideas, only to stare, bleary-eyed, at the inside of the refrigerator. "I'm too tired to cook," she said. "Why don't we just order pizza tonight?" She didn't need to ask twice; Nathan passed her the telephone before the sentence had fully emerged.

As they waited for the pizza, Shelley and Ken sorted the day's purchases, and the kids ran off to play. A few minutes later, Anna came rushing into the room crying. "I lost Manny Monkey!"

"I'm sure it's around here somewhere," answered Ken.

"No, Daddy!" she wailed. "I took it with me when we went shopping. We *have* to go back and find it—it was my *favorite*! And it's a limited first-edition retired premium one! It's worth, like . . . a million dollars!"

"You have tons of those little beanbag animals, honey. Next time, don't take your toys along to the mall."

Tears flooded her face. "You *have* to get me another one!"

"Anna!" interrupted her mother. "We can't just run out and replace everything you lose. Money doesn't grow on trees, you know!"

The Hidden Message

"Money may not grow on trees, but it spits right out of the automatic teller machine. There's an endless supply available for shopping, fast-food lunches, pizza for dinner, and a million of whatever constitutes the latest fad."

Think About It

We are always teaching our children—even if we don't realize a lesson is in progress. Every minute of every day we spend in our children's company is a demonstration of what we believe, and children learn well by example. This is particularly true in the arena of family finances. As we go about our days, we don't realize that our children are forming concepts about money based on what they see and hear. From a child's viewpoint, objects they need and want materialize out of nowhere. They have no opportunity to connect our purchases with the jobs we work, the taxes we pay, the mortgages and bills that worry our minds in quiet moments.

We pass up opportunities to teach our kids about money when we answer their requests for material goods by saying, "We can't afford it," or "We're not buying it today," without explaining the reasons behind our decisions. When we usher them off to a table at the fast-food restaurant, they don't see money changing hands and have no concept of the meal's cost. And value being relative, can small children understand the difference between twenty cents and twenty dollars without our putting it into perspective for them? To many kids, a shiny piece of copper is more appealing than a wrinkly green crumple of paper.

Money, value, cost, and the daily decisions we must make about all three: they're a mystery to our kids, one they will not solve easily on their own. In the interest of fostering healthy, productive ideas about material things, what they can and cannot do for us, and how we go about attaining them, it behooves us to reveal the realities to our kids in ordinary ways on a daily basis.

Changes You Can Make

You have many ways at your disposal to teach children. Begin with a simple self-directive: "I need to teach my kids about money, and I'll find opportunities every day to do it." Once you start, you'll be amazed at how many opportunities appear!

When you're purchasing a product or service, take a minute to tell your child how much you are paying. To make the amount more meaningful, put it in terms of your child's allowance or a favorite toy. For example, "Our lunch today cost twenty dollars— that's the same as four months of your allowance." Or, "The groceries I'm buying cost $100. That's the same as we paid for your bike." Can you see that your child may suddenly be more thoughtful when he asks for that second bag of fries? Imagine his shock when you explain that the new hot water tank you had to install cost the equivalent of 100 months of his allowance! Suddenly, these creature comforts don't just "materialize" anymore; they begin to have an understandable value in your child's mind.

When your daughter is compiling her holiday wish list and asks for that deluxe new doll set with hand-sewn clothes and period furniture, resist the urge to say, "We can't afford it." This only implies that if you had $600 lying around, you'd be delighted to buy one for her. Instead, pull out a catalog and show her that you could purchase holiday gifts for your entire extended family for that same amount of money.

When you've emptied your pockets or purse of change, don't just toss the coins into a drawer. This conveys to your child that a little bit of money isn't of value. Instead, save the coins in a jar, and when it's full, exchange the coins for cash to take the family

to the movies, showing that even sm
add up over time.

   When your child makes a request
cally buy for him, make him think r
by giving him a choice. "Sure, I coul
week for you. Or, you could skip a
could give you the three dollars towa
"We could stop for an ice cream cone and eat just one today, or
we could get the ingredients at the grocery store and have enough
for three ice cream cones each." Suddenly, your kids may be a little more aware of the value of those many incidentals that you
automatically purchase.

   It's also important to teach our children the joy of giving,
starting from a young age. If they see their own family purchasing all the goods that they need and want but never see money
going toward helping others less fortunate, they may assume that
charity has no place in their lives. Simple examples in action, such
as letting a child put coins in a collection box or including a few
gifts on your shopping trip for a church's holiday toy drive, can
send a message to your children that goes to the heart. Doing
these deeds during the holiday season also helps your children
understand that holidays are not just for making wish lists and
gathering presents, but also for sharing and caring about other
human beings.

   Give your children an allowance along with a few guidelines
and restrictions. (For example, allowances cannot be spent on
candy or toys that you deem inappropriate.) Help the kids create
a budget, but then let them learn how to make financial decisions.
They will make some poor ones, but over time, those mistakes
will lead to successes. For instance, if your child chooses to spend
his entire allowance on a new CD, then remembers that school
T-shirts are available for purchase, resist the urge to just throw
money at him. Instead, seize the opportunity to teach a lesson:
"Well, sometimes we choose to spend our money on one thing—

D—which means there isn't any for something else we'd
T-shirt. Those are money decisions we have to make."

your child has a desire for something special—a new bike,
-line skates, a guitar—don't grouse about his always wanting
something. Don't run out and buy it for him, either. Instead, sit
down with him and discuss the prospect of this latest treasure.
Validate his wish for new possessions: it's normal and acceptable
to want something special now and then. Tell him how much you
will be willing to chip in (a half, a third), and help him formulate
a plan to earn the rest. He'll learn some of the valuable lessons we
so need to teach: how to make a wise buying decision, how to
save, how to want some material things without letting "want"
consume one's soul, how to choose which of those "wants" to pursue and how to let the rest go. And after the purchase, because
he's been so personally involved, he'll likely treat the item with
much more respect than if it had just "appeared."

All of these ideas will help your children learn the real value of
money and give them a foundation for a stronger financial future.

2

Messages of Thoughtfulness and Kindness

Casual Remarks

It's a curious affliction: the tendency to talk about one's children in the most brutally honest and hurtful ways without realizing that the cherished subjects of the offensive comments are listening to every word. Right now, you may be saying to yourself, "This never happens to me." Perhaps. Perhaps not. I think that there's a good chance you'll see yourself in at least one of the following examples.

Unloading a cart full of Cheerios, macaroni-and-cheese, and hot dogs at the grocery store's checkout counter, a harried mother chats animatedly to the cashier. ". . . Only one more week 'til summer vacation, then the kids will be home all day. I can already hear the bickering! I don't know how I'll manage to live through the next few months! Want to buy two kids, cheap?" The cashier laughs and shakes her head, "Oh, no, thanks; I have my own! I know what you mean! I'm already waiting for next September!" In their supposedly innocent, lighthearted banter, neither one notices the shopper's two children standing right beside her, listening quietly to every hurtful word. Neither one notices a pair of small eyes cast downward just so, or a nervous little cough.

Consider Amir's situation as he walks through the door after another grueling day of work. His joyful, eager children run for Daddy, but Mom spies him coming in before they have their chance to pounce. And the daily gripe session begins. "I am *so* glad you're home. I need five minutes of peace and quiet. These kids drove me crazy all day! Abdi and Sheida have been like wild animals. They were fighting in the living room and knocked over the potted fern. Aria has been acting like a two-year-old—having temper tantrums over every little thing. The washing machine is broken again, and I have four stacks of kids' dirty clothes piled up in the laundry room . . ." Quietly and unnoticed, three dispirited children fade into the background of the family room and turn on the TV.

Then there's Megan, chatting on the phone with her best friend. As usual, the conversation turns to the daily goings-on with their children. Megan dramatically relates how annoyed she was with Kyle at baseball this morning. "I was so embarrassed," she groans. "The second time Kyle struck out, he stomped his foot like a baby and threw his helmet on the ground. You'd think he was five years old instead of fifteen!" She chuckles. "I think adolescent hormones are taking over." Meanwhile, said adolescent is just a few feet away, pretending to review his homework—but in actuality suffering from the blow of listening to his mother toss off his very real pain as if it were some big joke.

Many parents slip into the same type of unfortunate conversation as that of a mother and father who hailed me after a recent parenting lecture. They were in a frenzy to talk with me, bemoaning their three-year-old's latest behavior problems. "Molly's been a good girl until recently. It's as if we've entered the terrible twos a bit late. She's just no fun anymore. She's constantly yelling 'No!' to us, and she won't listen to a word we say. We've tried to be patient, but she's pushed us to the end of our rope!" I glance down to see a little three-year-old (Molly, perhaps?) clinging to her father's leg. But she's only three, and she doesn't understand what they're saying; this couldn't possibly hurt her.

Or so we think.

The Hidden Message

"I can talk about you all I want, and since you're just a child, you're not listening to what I say anyway. You're not worthy of the same respect I'd give another adult. Besides, this is how I *really* feel about you, and I don't care about your feelings—you're just a kid, so your feelings aren't important."

Think About It

If you don't believe that your children hear your casual remarks, try this: as you chat with a friend or your spouse, casually slip a question into the middle of your conversation—something along the lines of, "Do you think we should round up the kids and take them out for ice cream?" Be ready to hop into the car when you hear a chorus of "Yes!" from the four corners of the house.

Children do not always react outwardly to what they hear. However, if you could see into their hearts, you would find a record of every careless word, every thoughtless action, every adult laugh that here, in the most tender and vulnerable of places, was not considered so funny. Here you would also find significant—and often, inappropriate—meaning attached to these products of childhood internalization. Children struggle through the growing-up process, and along the way, they question who they are and what their meaning is to this world and to their parents. A parent's potent words, and the multitude of other comments, gestures, and actions, help a child paint a picture of who he really is, and how important he is in this world. How tragic for that child if, despite the love and pride that we really feel, they conclude that they're not the masterpiece we envision!

Changes You Can Make

Given the extreme importance of your words, it makes good sense to choose them carefully. From now on, if your child is within hearing distance, assume that he may be listening—and don't say anything *about* him that you wouldn't say *to* him.

If you see a bit of yourself in the previous examples, you're no different from most other parents. But that doesn't mean that this behavior needn't cease. Such a simple change could have a very positive impact on your children's lives. As you talk about your children—and let's face it, they're among our favorite topics—pay attention to how those words sound from your child's point of view. If you think that what you're saying, or about to say, can be construed as hurtful or embarrassing, *stop*. Talk about something else.

If you're not sure if what you're saying has a negative impact or not, ask yourself how you would feel if you overheard someone talking about you in those words. Or you can ask yourself, "If I were talking about my boss/spouse/best friend to another person, with the object of my comments listening, would I ever say such a thing?" If your answer is a mortified laugh, then stop in midsentence and rephrase your comments to be more complimentary, if you find them crucial to the conversation.

Better yet, find something shining and wonderful to say about your child, and be sure your child hears it. That type of "casual remark" can yield life-enhancing benefits to your children. It may help them compose a more wonderful vision of themselves. An image that they can carry with them for the rest of their lives.

Where Are Your Manners?

Scene 1 I'm in line at the grocery store on a busy shopping day. In front of me, a teenager leans on the handle of a cart, absent-mindedly humming and rocking the cart slowly back and forth. Ahead of him is his father, leafing through a magazine and sighing audibly as the woman in front of him hands over a stack of coupons to the cashier. As the line inches forward, the teenager, in his own private world, moves forward also, but just a dot too quickly—and predictably, scuffs his father's heels with the cart. Obviously annoyed, Dad admonishes his son, looking around to confirm that those nearby notice how he demands good behavior from his offspring. "Pay attention!" he nearly yells. "You rammed that cart right into my heels!" He then none too gently moves his son out of the way to take control of the cart, catching my eye with a weary expression. "Kids!" he says with a heavy sigh, as his scarlet-faced son slinks toward the front door to wait apart from his father.

Scene 2 Several of us are waiting in a shopping mall's elevator as the doors slide open; in steps a mother and her young daughter. The mother presses the button for their desired destination and steps back. Her little girl pushes forward and bangs on three or four more buttons. Mother stops her just as she's ready to depress the red emergency button, grabbing her arm and scolding her loudly and tersely. "What are you doing? Leave those alone, and keep your hands to yourself. Now, *behave*." The rest of us cringe.

Scene 3 I'm enjoying a day out with my kids. From somewhere close by, I hear the fitful exclamations of a frustrated child. Turning toward the source of the sounds, I spy a little girl struggling to get her ball out of a blackberry bush. I wander over and, after a bit of a struggle myself, manage to free the ball. Her mother walks up just in time to see her daughter yank the ball from my hands and turn away. Mom steps in, forcefully turning her daughter to face me. "Where are your manners, young lady? Don't be so rude! You need to say 'thank you' when someone helps you. Now, you say 'thank you' or we'll go home right now." The girl, barely six, mumbles unintelligibly through the tears that welled up first with the frustration of the stuck ball and then with the anguish of a public flogging.

Scene 4 While running errands, I meet a friend I've not seen in years; her two children are standing beside her. When I say hello to them, they look down at their feet and ignore me, shifting around shyly. Dismayed by their behavior, my friend laughs and says, "Sorry about that. They obviously left their manners at home today." They steal a glance at each other, feeling insignificant and unimportant to the conversation passing above their heads.

Scene 5 We're at a pizza party in our elementary school's gym. Families fill picnic tables end-to-end. Beside us, a boy chews his pizza noisily enough for all to hear—and amuses himself by opening his mouth to show everyone the source of the cacophony. His father is appalled. "Chris! That's disgusting! Stop acting like a baby, and use your manners!" The din of the families around Chris comes to a stunned halt as they stare at the boy, who wishes the gym floor would swallow him up whole.

The Hidden Message

"While I expect *you* to use good manners, I certainly don't have to use them myself."

Think About It

We all want polite children. And right or wrong, whether we admit it or not, we sometimes judge other parents by the rudeness of their kids. So it is that we parents often jump in so quickly to correct our kids' bad manners that we don't realize how our words will be perceived—by our children, and by anyone else within earshot. Sometimes we're so consumed by our good intentions, so caught up in our well-meaning strategies, that we miss the very rudeness of the correction itself! Unfortunately, our presentation teaches as much as, if not more than, our words themselves.

The foregoing examples all occurred in public places, in full view of others. Having caught their children in a transgression, these parents attempt to demonstrate their effectiveness by swiftly and firmly correcting the mistake. The intention and the concept are good, but the delivery engenders more embarrassment (for both the child and the bystanders) than audience approval.

These occurrences are not limited to outings, either. In the secure confines of home, parents often upbraid their children so quickly and sharply that there, too, they miss the impact of the delivery. "Give that back to your sister—right now!" "When you learn to use good manners, *then* I'll listen to you!" "That was *rude*!" "That's disgusting. Don't be such a *pig*!" In these cases, the child may latch on to the parent's harsh words more than the intended message.

Changes You Can Make

When your children display bad manners—and they *will*—suppress the knee-jerk reaction that adds your own bad manners to the show. It's so much more polite to take your child aside and voice your corrections privately, delivering these admonitions in the spirit of teaching rather than reprimanding. When your own presentation is polite and encouraging, you may find your children actually learning the intended lesson through your example.

Keep in mind that a child is not born with good manners. They are an acquired skill. Often, poor manners may be not intentional misbehavior but childish naïveté—in which case, you have an opportunity to teach the correct behavior gently if you refrain from mindless snapping. Likewise, poor manners also may be displays of age-appropriate behavior. All young children spill milk, splatter ketchup, leave crumbs, and wax incoherent when introduced to a stranger.

How do you make corrections politely? Try rephrasing your child's comment the way you'd like to hear it. "What I'd like to hear you say is . . ." Or try pointing out the impropriety of the action and then explain the proper response. "When an adult is talking to you, it's impolite to look away. It's good manners to look a person in the eye and respond to questions in some way." You may even firmly remind children of the good manners they already have but are not using. "You know that it's bad manners to show everyone the food in your mouth. Please chew with your mouth closed."

Another technique especially valuable with younger children is the preventive approach. In advance of a social situation, take time to recap what behavior will be expected. You may even want to preview the event with a short role-play so that your child, and you, can be confident that he knows the right ways to behave. And when your children do use good manners, praise them! Build them up, let them know they've made you proud, and you'll promote a repeat performance.

Remember: our children learn most by watching adult behavior and modeling it. Your own mannerly behavior may just be enough to get your children mimicking you in the most becoming way.

Danny the Disrespectful Kid

Danny arrives home after school the way he usually does: with muddy footprints, abandoned backpack, half-eaten lunch, and jacket trailing him on the floor. His mother looks up at him, making that "tsk" sound that only mothers can produce quite that way, followed by a weary sigh. "Geez, Danny, why do you have to come in like a tornado?" Danny mocks her the way he always does when she makes this comment. Whirling around, he knocks several articles off the counter en route to his first destination, which is, of course, the refrigerator.

As his mother picks up the first wave of his debris from the floor, Danny busily creates another as he roots through the refrigerator, upending yogurt containers, spilling juice from a pitcher, bruising apples, and leaving leftovers uncovered. This messy expedition yields a muffin—and a complaint that his mother never buys anything good to eat. He devours half the muffin in one bite, scattering crumbs over the floor with a cough. As his mom reaches down to scoop up the crumbs, he sees she's none too pleased, but that doesn't faze him as he blithely rains more crumbs down on the floor.

She hates this unmannerly behavior, hates the fact that he, sated by his muffin feast, will turn up his nose at a dinner she spent hours preparing. "Danny! Can't you see that I'm making dinner?" she asks. "I wish you wouldn't eat a bunch of snacks right now."

Through a mouth filled with muffin number two, Danny mumbles something that sounds like "Whatever."

"Honey, did you get the book you need for your book report?" Mom asks.

Ignoring her question, Danny asks, "Did you get me new shin guards for soccer?"

"No," his mother responds. "I haven't had time to get to the sports shop."

Danny looks disgusted. "Geesh, Mom, whaddya *do* all day around here? Watch soaps? You better go *now*, 'cause I need those shin guards."

His mother glances at the clock and shakes her head. "It's too late now, but we can go after dinner." He takes another bite of yet another muffin. She explodes, "I asked you not to eat anything else!" She tries to retrieve it, but Danny dances away from her, holding his prize high. They both know that his recent growth spurt put the muffin way out of her reach. "Danny, stop it!" his mother complains.

"Danny, *stop* it!" he mimics in a grating, singsong voice.

Heaving a resigned sigh, she decides it's not worth a fight and lets it pass. Instead, she resumes the so-called conversation where it had left off. "So, did you get the book?"

Danny peels back the muffin paper. "I already said 'Yeah.' Whatsa matter—hearing aid need new batteries?"

His mother answers this rude remark the way she answers all of them. "Watch your mouth!" Especially disturbed by his recent desire to find humor in her hearing aid, she adds, "You *know* I don't appreciate your talking to me like that." The only sound in the kitchen then comes from Danny, who is absentmindedly rumpling muffin papers.

Danny casts a look at his mom. "Yo! I could use some milk with this . . ."

His mother glares at him, the unspoken words hanging in the air: *What do you say?* She can't believe that at his age she would still have to remind him to say "please."

Danny's smart enough to read her warning sign but not wise enough to understand the social impact of his rudeness. A sarcastic and belabored "Plllleeeeeease" spills out just below his wrinkled nose. Mom presents him a glass of milk, napkin, and plate. "I *only* asked for *milk*," Danny grumbles. He tosses little muffin paper basketballs across the room toward the trash can, decidedly blowing the three-pointers and littering the floor. As his mother cleans up crumbs and papers, she looks sideways at him and suggests, "Why don't you start reading the book until dinner's ready?"

Danny rolls his eyes. "I just got home. Gimme a *break* here."

His mother takes a deep breath and persists, "But, honey, you're already behind on it . . ."

Danny gives her a look that says he thinks she's stupid. "Would you shut *up* with the book already?"

Shocked and finally, deeply humiliated, his mother stiffens from the sting of her son's meanness. "Don't talk to me that way, young man. I want you to sit down and read some of that book. I don't know why you always wait until the last minute to get started on your projects. Then you stay up 'til midnight trying to finish, and you end up rushing . . ." She glances up to see Danny's back as he's walking out of the room.

On his way out, spoken in a loud voice obviously for her benefit, she hears "Yada-yada-yada," followed by the din of the TV.

"Danny!" she calls, "don't sit down in front of that TV yet. Come set the table!"

"Why do *I* always have to do it?" he yells to no one in particular. And that is the end of that. From the volume he's turned up on the TV, it's obvious to his mother that *she'll* be setting the table again tonight, and that all discussion on *any* subject is over. Mom yanks a pile of plates from the counter and slams them onto the table, complaining (to herself, I suppose), "I don't know why you can't be more polite and helpful . . ."

The Hidden Message

"You can be as disrespectful to me as you want; you'll suffer no consequences whatsoever. I'll do nothing to influence you to change your behavior, so we can continue on this way for the rest of our lives."

Think About It

It's offensive to hear a child act in such rude and disrespectful ways toward a parent. But the sad fact is that even good kids pick up this behavior from their peers, movies, and TV shows. Many parents are distressed at seeing this behavior in their own children, and they mistakenly believe themselves powerless to change it.

Most parents start off on the right foot—teaching toddlers to say "please" and "thank you." Over time, however, tedious reminders and busy schedules interfere with continuing lessons. A few rude or insulting remarks slip by uncorrected, and soon an unpleasant pattern emerges—a pattern that gets more difficult to break as the child ages. It's like a smudge on the wall: if you walk by it often enough, you cease to notice it. And the longer it stays, the harder it is to remove.

The startling reality is that the disrespect itself is not the problem here, but merely a symptom of a much greater difficulty: on the child's part, a failure to understand expectations and the hierarchy of authority, and on the parent's part, a failure to communicate those expectations.

Changes You Can Make

The first inroad to correcting this disagreeable situation is to establish a firm and proper hierarchy of authority. In other words, it's high time to let your kid know you're the boss! To do this, first believe it yourself, and give yourself permission to be in charge. Absorb the truth that, for your child to grow into a responsible, civil, and successful adult, you must train, guide, and direct during the growing years. You have just a few short years to establish a foundation upon which he will build his entire life.

Once you have decided to take control, begin by establishing clear expectations and rules for your child to follow. As Danny so painfully illustrates, if you have allowed your child to be rude and disrespectful without correction, you have established clear expectations—all the wrong ones! Take your child a few giant steps back to toddlerhood and require that he—whatever his age—say "please," "thank you," and "may I?" When he doesn't, avoid that annoying cliché "What do you say?" Instead, rephrase your child's request in the form you'd like to hear it: "Danny, what I'd like to hear you say is, 'May I please have some milk?'" If he doesn't repeat his request in the way you've asked, let him eat his muffin dry (if you decide to let him keep the muffin at all). The key is to be indefatigable. Do not let one single disrespectful comment slide.

Let your child know what you're up to. Admit that you have allowed his behavior to get out of control, but declare that it stops, and it stops *today*. Discuss your expectations, and make yourself perfectly clear. "I expect you to be polite and respectful to me and your dad every single time you talk to us."

Once you've established clear expectations and pleasantly corrected him for a week or two, you can take the next step. Make a list of your child's privileges—freedom to use the TV, the telephone, and his bicycle, for example. The list can include dessert, rides to friends' homes, visits to and from friends, and the like. (The list could be endless.) Number the privileges on the list, and cross off items with each offense. Then be sure to follow through with removal of privileges for the remainder of that week. Start each week with a fresh list and a fresh start.

Another reason to get a kid like Danny on the right track is that he may be acting tough, but on the inside he's struggling with the knowledge that he really shouldn't be treating people, especially his parents, in such rude ways. Most kids know that what they are doing is wrong, and they may wonder why no one is correcting them. Over time, this voice of conscience will fade, and the child will accept the rude demeanor as normal.

One final but important point: Make certain that *you* are using your best manners when you talk to your child. "Do what I say, not what I do" is not an effective parenting philosophy. Your actions as an appropriate role model are imperative to correcting this undesirable display.

The Dentist

Dori opened the curtains to the morning sun and sat on the edge of her daughter's bed. Her usually chipper early bird just slid deeper under the covers. "Come on, Naomi, time to get up!" Naomi groaned and announced that she wasn't getting up today. "And why not?" Dori asked, although she knew the answer.

From somewhere under the covers came a tiny, frightened voice, one that under normal circumstances could be heard from blocks away. "I don't want to go to the dentist. I'm scared."

"Oh, Naomi! There's nothing to be scared of, honey. It's nothing to have *baby* teeth pulled. The dentist said that it won't even hurt, because baby teeth don't have much of a root at all. It will be over before you know it." Dori tried to fight the notion that her daughter wasn't as strong or brave as she should be.

Naomi stalled. She groaned, she squirmed, she stretched—but in the end, she finally crawled out of bed. She felt cold, despite the morning's warmth. After getting dressed, she came into the kitchen and poured her usual Paul Bunyan–size bowl of cereal. Dori walked in just as Naomi was about to add the milk. "Stop!" she called out. "Remember, the dentist said no breakfast this morning!"

Naomi's bottom lip began to quiver. "It's not fair, Mom!" she protested. "It's bad enough I have to go to the dentist. Now I can't even eat my own breakfast?"

Dori hurriedly scooped the cereal back into the box. "You know it's for your own good. You need to follow the doctor's instructions."

"But I'm hungry!" Naomi shouted.

"Well, it doesn't help to get all upset about it." Dori continued in a calm and understanding voice, "Go brush your hair and your teeth and get ready to go." An exceptionally loud clomping of feet signaled Naomi's exit. Dori rolled her eyes.

A few minutes later, they were in the car bound for the dentist's office. After Naomi had changed the radio station a dozen times, Dori finally reached over and turned it off. "Calm down, honey!"

"I can't," Naomi whined. "How long is this gonna take? What time will I get to school?"

"I'm not sure how long the procedure takes. But the dentist said you'd be taking the rest of the day off to relax and recover."

"No way!" Naomi complained, "I'm supposed to meet Sara and Julia at the playground for recess! We were going to try out the new tire swing! If I'm not there, they'll get mad at me."

Her mom smiled at her. "Of course, they won't be mad at you. That would be silly. Just tell them about your teeth being pulled."

Naomi contemplated that for a moment. Then she gathered herself, straightened her back, and matter-of-factly announced that she would not be having any teeth pulled today.

Her Mom laughed. "Oh, yes you are!"

Naomi tensed in frustration. She felt like crawling out of her skin. "It's not funny, Mom . . ." Naomi's bottom lip was quivering again, the way it did when she was a toddler confronted by something she neither understood nor felt comfortable with. "It *is* gonna hurt."

Dori took a deep breath and glanced at her daughter, "Honey, it's OK. I really trust this dentist. He does good work. It will be over quickly, and remember, he said it probably won't hurt at all."

Naomi mumbled the word "probably," and her shoulders hunched as she slid deeper into her seat, watching the world rush by her window. She imagined that behind every window of every house they passed was a girl with more bravery and better teeth than she had. What was wrong with her? She was worried about baby stuff. And suddenly, she felt very, very small.

The Hidden Message

"Don't be so foolish! The emotions you feel are silly and inappropriate. *I'll* tell you how you should feel; and if you don't, then something's wrong with you."

Think About It

"Stop crying; it doesn't hurt." "Everything will be OK." "You have nothing to worry about—you're just a kid." "You'll do fine on the test." Such natural adult responses! But your child is likely thinking: "But it *does* hurt!" "I *am* worried!" "It's *not* OK!" Children, like adults, *do* feel what they feel; telling them that they *don't* just confuses and frustrates them; it doesn't make the feeling go away. In fact, the child will feel wholly misunderstood and lonely in her fear, and the emotional monster that has been created then feeds on itself. In addition, every human being has a different tolerance level for pain. What "doesn't hurt" for one person may hurt a lot for another. It's impossible to judge another person's pain—physical or emotional.

So, if denying your children's feelings doesn't help, what about explaining away the problem or giving sage advice? Neither of these helps, either. Your child is so immersed in her feelings that, while you're busy explaining or advising, she's busy trying to convince you of her very real concerns. The result is that you both talk at, instead of to, one another, and neither of you really hears the other.

The problem is that we view child-size concerns through adult eyes. But seeing the picture is a matter of proportion: a child's problems are relative to her size. Remember how huge, for example, a countertop seemed when you were a kid? That's because you were so much smaller. When you grew above that countertop, you forgot the frustration of reaching for a snack placed there for you when you couldn't even see it. Our fears are like that. And fears of one type or another are always with us—only their scale changes. Our countertops simply grow higher as we become older and more experienced, but the feelings of fear are still there.

Changes You Can Make

Could the answer for Dori be as simple as acknowledging her daughter's feelings? Letting her know that her feelings are real—solely by virtue of their being felt—and that her concerns, her pain, and her worry are normal? Yes, indeed! The best response when children are fearful is validation.

Next time your child approaches you with pain, fear, or worry, stifle the urge to respond in those usual unhelpful ways, such as denying the feelings, minimizing the fear, or waving away your child's concern. What your child wants most from you at a time like that is to have you *listen* to her concerns and acknowledge her feelings. "Yes, honey, I know you're feeling scared. Even grown-ups don't like to go to the dentist." Once her feelings are accredited, she'll be much more likely to hear your words of explanation or advice which, in turn, may actually help soothe her. If you deny her feelings, she'll feel compelled to prove to you, and to herself, that they are valid in order to save face. Once you give her feelings validity, you can help her understand and surmount them. You can then help her develop strategies to mitigate the fear or pain that she's struggling with. The ideas you offer, once she feels safe enough to express her fears, are the foundation for strategies that she'll adapt later in life when confronted by fears of a more adult proportion. Plus, when you help her understand and identify her emotions, you will help her to better understand herself, and to trust her own perceptions about life.

There's another inherent benefit to this approach: if she doesn't feel ridiculed even when she expresses fears that she herself may think are a little unwarranted, she'll be more likely to come to you for the big stuff. She'll be more likely to turn to you rather than to inappropriate, and perhaps dangerous, people and situations. You'll be the safe port in a storm that she'll need later, a place she can go where she's sure to be understood and comforted no matter how silly—or serious—her fear seems.

3

Messages of Annoyance and Anger

Yelling or Hugging?

"Yesterday was one of those days." Claire sighed and then paused, as if she were reliving the day. "Everything Joshua did was grating on my nerves. It started as soon as he woke up and came downstairs. The first thing he did was open a new box of cereal and dump it all over the kitchen floor! Then he just stepped all over the mess and poured half a gallon of milk into his bowl. Then he was climbing on the counter—which he knows he's not allowed to do. Next thing you know, he's coloring on the kitchen table. The table! No paper in sight! It seemed as if I was yelling at him every five minutes. My nerves were raw, and I was counting the minutes until bedtime—and then I caught Josh cleaning his muddy truck in the bathroom sink! We've been through this before, and he *knows* he's not supposed to bring his muddy trucks into the house.

"As I approached the bathroom, all I could see was the muddy water dripping down the counter into a big puddle on the floor. I stomped into the bathroom, took a deep breath, and prepared to give him yet another high-volume lecture. I was so angry that I was actually shaking. I understood for the first time why even the best of parents suddenly find themselves grabbing their children and spanking them. I took hold of Joshua's arm, and inadvertently, I glanced in the mirror.

"What I saw shocked me. I looked like a savage! My face was red, veins protruding on my neck and eyes wild with what appeared to be—but was not—hatred! This, I thought, all because of a muddy toy truck! It seemed so absurd that I suddenly found myself devoid of all my anger. Since I had Joshua's arm in my grip, I pulled him to me. I wrapped both my arms around him, hugging him for all I was worth and crying for that woman I saw in the mirror. Wordlessly, instinctively, Josh wrapped his tiny arms around me and hugged me back. After a few minutes, I glanced at the mirror—but this time, instead of the out-of-control, angry mother I'd seen a moment ago, I saw my sweet, innocent little boy, cheeks smeared with mud, arms straining with the effort to hold me in this moment. I saw Love."

The Hidden Message

"I have a choice between yelling at you and hugging you. Because I love you, I will try to choose the hugging—and I will allow you to show me the good in myself in so doing."

Think About It

In every parent's life are days when everything your child does seems wrong, wrong, wrong—when he keeps breaking the rules and disrupting the peace. At times like these, it's so easy to punctuate the air with corrections, directions, and reminders. Every misbehavior, every mistake, every childish action builds on the one before, and soon we allow our anger to rule our emotions.

Claire was lucky. Somehow she was able to get control of her anger before it got control of her. The result is not always so positive. Often, a very unpleasant scene erupts from our uncontrolled anger and our distinct lack of purpose. Caught up in an angry rush of adrenaline, we *react* instead of taking action. It's a domino effect, predictable and uncomfortable: we get angry; we react thoughtlessly; we punish, yell, swear, or worse; the child cries; the anger builds. Banished from our sight, the child sulks off to plan revenge or to despair over the unfairness of life. And we are left to recover ever so slowly from our anger—suffering regret, sadness, embarrassment, and shame. It's an oft-repeated play that gets bad reviews from audiences all the time, from every seat in the house.

Changes You Can Make

As much as we wish it were not so, anger is as much a part of parenting as changing diapers. There will always be misbehavior, mistakes, and childish foolishness. There will always be things that we must get our children to do or to stop doing. There will always be unfulfilled expectations and outside pressures and stresses that reduce our tolerance level. But there is always love. And where there is love, there is always the motivation to improve, on all sides.

We can accept the reality of anger—but we should resist falling into the negative patterns that it can so easily create. Learning how to recognize and control our anger is crucial to maintaining a peaceful family life.

The first key to anger control is to shed the behaviors that fuel it. The most dangerous of these lurk in our own thoughts—negative, unforgiving, black-and-white thoughts such as: "Why is he doing this to me?" "She should know better!" "This is horrible!" "I can't take another minute of this!" We further pump up the volume on our anger by allowing ourselves the luxury of emotional tunnel vision: we see, hear, and understand nothing beyond that which is creating our anger, thus magnifying and distorting it.

It follows, then, that controlling our own thoughts is a logical course to pursue in staying even-keeled at these times. Promise yourself right now that, next time you feel your adrenaline rise, you will take a deep breath and repeat a calming mantra. Something like, "She's just a toddler." Or, "I can handle this." Or, "This too shall pass." Take a minute to look at your child, and try to find the love that is hidden there. Remind yourself that she won't be little for long, and someday—trust me—you will miss this period of time.

If this doesn't pull you out of the whirlpool of anger, your next move is to put some space between you and your child. If that child is young, put him in his crib, in his playpen, or in the care of another adult. If the child can walk and talk, it's best if you avoid the time-out confrontation right now; instead, control what you can—your own behavior—and walk away to a quiet spot in your bedroom, bathroom, or backyard. Think of this as your own time-out, a time for you to gather your wits, settle yourself down, and plan an appropriate response to the situation. This allows you to return to your child with a level head and a purposeful plan on which you can follow through without the fog of anger disrupting your vision.

Like Claire, you'll likely discover that a change in your mind can cause a change in your heart.

You Two!

The first pain comes with the first sip of coffee—which Nadine had *hoped* to enjoy in peace—and hits her somewhere in the middle of her stomach, rapidly ascending to become the day's first migraine. Moments later, the source of her suffering enters the kitchen. Nadine squeezes her eyes shut and covers her ears, but she can't blot out the annoying and persistent whine assaulting her from two directions: "Mom! Ryan took my soccer ball and he won't give it back!"

"I did not! Joey's lying! It's mine!"

"It's mine! Make him give it back!"

Nadine droops and shivers from head to toe. She snatches up the ball and moans, "Can't you two *ever* get along?"

Sans one soccer ball, the boys trek into the family room to watch cartoons. The atmosphere in the house is now like that which follows a thunderstorm on a thick, hot summer day—muted and exhausted of force but edged with heat that will eventually build up the thunderheads once again. Nadine monitors the radar screen at its first rumble and listens helplessly as the storm rages anew. Shouts fill the house, and Joey becomes a cloudburst, crying so hard that Nadine can't make out his accusing words. She drags herself into the room just in time to see the boys on the floor, wrestling over the remote control.

"Stop it!" she shouts. "Why must you two always act like wild animals?!"

Banished from the family room, the boys and their storm loom over the computer desk. Nadine goes upstairs to sort the day's laundry but trudges back down with heavy footfalls when another conflict flares. Could they be at it again? Sure enough, she pokes her head around the corner to see the boys fighting over their computer game—which, in itself, was a battle scene. They were fighting over the *fighting*. "I can't ever leave you two alone, not even for a minute!" she complains.

Whether attended or not, the bickering and fighting continue throughout the morning. By lunchtime, Nadine is wild with frustration and beyond all the patient, positive, ego-affirming strategies she'd once vowed to use on the kids she'd someday have. As the boys sit eating—with respective elbows, feet, and other assorted appendages separated to prevent turf wars—she launches into what she intends as a motherly lecture but comes off as a general dressing down the troops. "I don't know *what* is the matter with you two. You fight constantly, and you never even try to get along. It seems as if you *can't* play together for even a minute! I just don't know what to do anymore. Maybe you should just stay away from each other."

The Hidden Message

"I believe that you will always be enemies, and that you don't— and never will—have the skills and intelligence to get along. There's no point in your trying to improve. You're hopeless."

Think About It

It's a common human response. When driven to the brink by the behavior of those around us, we resort to describing it in absolute terms: "You always . . ." "You never . . ." "You are . . ." This kind of characteriziation isn't good for marriages or friendships—but it's especially destructive in parenthood, since our efforts are directed toward a future that these words doom.

The words Nadine uses in her interactions with her children describe a specific negative existence and a hopeless future: "Can't you two ever get along?" "Why must you two always act like wild animals?!" "I can't leave you two alone, not even for a minute!" "You fight constantly, and you never even try to get along." Since Nadine is their mother, Ryan and Joey trust her and believe her. Over time, they begin to see themselves exactly as she describes them and, in the process, lose all motivation for even the weakest attempts at change. They risk becoming precisely what their mother fears: estranged adult siblings.

Changes You Can Make

Stop responding to your children with clichés and absolutes like *always* and *never*. Instead, think about the meaning of your words and their impact on your children's perception of themselves and their actions. Stop using absolute expressions to describe the negative behavior you want to eliminate. Replace those dangerous words with more helpful ones that describe behavior you *want* to see. For example, replace that tired old parental adage "How many times do I have to tell you?"—which both implies that your child has a lousy memory and invites a rhetorical response—with a sincere observation such as "I should have to tell you only one time." Replace the classic and useless remark "Why did you do that?" with something more constructive, such as "How are you going to solve this problem?" Eliminate rejoinders that make you sound like a victim, such as "Don't talk to me that way!" Turn the situation into a teaching experience with this helpful phrase, "What I'd like to hear you say is . . ." Moreover, plot your teaching strategies in this area *before* the situation saps you of your patience and ability to think clearly.

Just for fun, let's revise the script of Nadine's migraine-producing day, replacing her negative responses with ones that direct her children in a more positive way. The long-term impact of this change is obvious, as you will see:

"Mom! Ryan took my soccer ball and he won't give it back!"

"I did not! Joey's lying! It's mine!"

"It's mine! Make him give it back!"

Nadine unceremoniously takes the ball from Ryan, parks it on the floor, looks at her boys, and says, "I know the two of you can work this out. Why don't you guys sit right here and talk about it. You're very capable of solving this problem without me."

The boys retreat to the family room to watch TV. Moments later, shouts reverberate throughout the house, and Joey begins to cry. Nadine walks into the room just in time to see the boys wrestling over the remote control. Nadine turns off the TV, takes the remote, and places it on the cabinet, saying, "As soon as the two of you have a plan, you may turn the TV back on."

Nadine goes upstairs to sort the day's laundry. It doesn't take long for another tussle to begin. Nadine heads toward the sounds of battle coming from both the computer and its current operators. She pokes her head in to see the boys fighting over their computer game. "Maybe this isn't a good time for the computer. Why don't you guys find something else to do?"

Even though Nadine's comments have been helpful, ingrained habits do not change in one day. Sure enough, the bickering and fighting continue throughout the morning. By lunchtime, Nadine is exasperated. As the boys sit quietly, eating their lunch, she launches into a motherly lecture. "I know that the two of you can get along much better than you have been today. What can we do to make this afternoon more fun for all of us?" And for the rest of their lunchtime, the three of them discuss a plan for the remainder of the day.

As this example shows, a parent's words can indeed influence the direction of children's behavior, but sometimes, lighting on something positive to say is a nearly insurmountable challenge. And naturally, just using more constructive, productive language will not prevent bickering, whining, complaining, and misbehaving from ever recurring in your family. (If only it were so simple!) Your words, however, might just have a pleasant and cumulative effect on the overall atmosphere in your family; maybe, just maybe, your children's thinking about one another will reflect and take on your new attitude. And in the process, you'll garner more opportunities to teach your children the lessons of life so crucial to happy adulthood.

Chinese Water Torture–Child Style

Ed is busy changing the oil in his car when his daughter approaches. Tiffany is wearing her jacket and bicycle helmet as she walks her bike toward him. "Daddy, can I ride my bike over to Megan's house?"

Distracted, Ed shakes his head and mumbles, "Nope."

"Why not?" Tiffany asks.

Ed looks up. "'Cause we're going to have dinner in an hour, and I want you to stay home."

"But," Tiffany sputters, "I already have my helmet on, and I unlocked my bike."

With the common sense of an adult, Ed responds, "Well, put them away."

Tiffany doesn't move; instead, she watches Ed's oil-changing process for a few minutes. "Daddy?"

"Hmmm."

"If I go now, I can be back in an hour for dinner."

Ed pauses before answering. "I don't think so, honey. We have to leave right after dinner, so we have to eat on time. Last time you promised to be back, you were more than thirty minutes late. I want you to stay home."

But Tiffany has a solution to that problem, too. "I'll wear my watch. I can be back in time. I promise!"

Ed responds with a grunted "Uh, uh."

"I can have Tiffany's mom remind me when to go home."

Ed glances up at her. "That's what you said last time. The answer is no."

Tiffany is now rolling her bike back and forth beside the car. "But Dad-eee! It's summer vacation. I don't know why I can't do something fun!"

Ed smiles up at her. "Watching me change the oil is fun *and* educational!" He chuckles at his witty remark, the way parents do—and Tiffany rolls her eyes the way their children do.

A few more minutes tick by. "Daddy?"

"Hmmm?"

"Can I pleeeeze go? Just for forty-five minutes?" Tiffany takes advantage of her father's silence, cautiously optimistic that Ed is pondering her proposal. He's wearing down, and she can sense it. "I promise, promise, promise I'll be home in forty-five minutes. I really will." Ed is still quiet. ("Is he yielding, or ignoring me?" Tiffany wonders.) "Then I'll come home and help set the table. Ok? Pleeeeze, Daddy?"

Ed emits the sound of one defeated. "Ok. Go. But be back in forty-five minutes!" Tiffany, braced with the rush of victory, pedals off quickly.

The Hidden Message

"Of course, you can get me to change my mind. All you have to do is wheedle, beg, complain, plead, and be a major pest, until you get the answer you want."

Think About It

If a child is persistent and creative, she often can convince you that her argument is valid. She may have some good points, and you may actually agree with her. *However*, each and every time she succeeds in using this method to make you change your mind, she accumulates more experience and confidence in her ability to manipulate you. The parent's constant giving in creates a vicious cycle: The parent says no. The child questions. The parent says no. The child whines. The parent says no. The child negotiates. The parent says no. The child begs. The parent says *yes*. The child gains a victory. The victory propels the child to repeat the entire process the next time the parent says no . . . and the next . . . and the next. Children know their parents well. They can easily figure out if persistence will pay off with them or not, and the more practice they get, the better they get at deducing exactly how to persuade them to say *yes*.

The concept described here underlies the very reason Las Vegas and Reno are popular vacation spots. When people gamble, they are not successful 100 percent of the time, but each time they hit even a modest jackpot, it is incentive enough to come back and try again. So, there you have it: children respond to parental cave-ins just as vacationing gamblers respond to winning, gaining the motivation to continue the behavior that brings them success.

Changes You Can Make

The change required in this case is short and sweet and simple: when you say no, don't change your mind. Don't reinforce the wheedling, begging, whining, complaining, and pleading. Allow your child—and yourself—to get used to the premise that your word is final. And accept that your child will be unhappy on occasion as a consequence.

This plan is easier to adhere to if you circumvent the implied pressure to answer your child immediately. "Can Emily sleep over tonight?" Your knee-jerk response may be no, but if you say instead, "Give me a minute to think about it," you may verify in your own mind that no is the best answer, or you may resolve that it actually is a good night for a sleep-over. When you are more confident in your answer, you are less likely to be coerced into changing it.

Of course, there are incidences when a child's reasons do compel you to reverse your ruling. At such times, make it clear that you have done so because *you* have reevaluated the options and have revised your decision. But it's important that you choose when to make an exception, as opposed to being pushed into compromise against your better judgment by a cajoling child. Also, there is a big difference between a child using respectful reasoning to present her case versus protraction like the Chinese water torture demonstrated in this slice of life.

If you have already developed the vicious cycle of allowing your child to erode your will until you crack, and you've decided to change this pattern, get ready for a period of intensified emotions. Your child will at first wonder why her usual methods aren't working. Then, she'll assume that she must try harder to manipulate you. At this point, you determine the future. You can crumble and set yourself up for a lifetime of extraordinary battles. Or you can hold fast, stand your ground, grit your teeth, bite the bullet, and, well, you get the picture.

When you say no, mean it.

The Annoying New Neighbor

Taek glances out the window to see the new neighbor kid, Jeffrey, waltzing toward their front door. "Oh, no," Taek groans to his wife, "here he comes again . . ."

Olivia scrunches her face. On cue, an unmistakably screechy voice announces its owner's presence just inside the front door. "Sami!" the voice squawks. Olivia and Taek exchange hopeless looks. "Sami? You home?" Jeffrey's shrill voice can probably be heard across the street.

Taek's usually tolerant voice is tense with restraint as he sputters a complaint to his wife. "Do you think the kid would learn to knock? You believe this kid, Olivia? He just walks in here like he owns the place! And does he have to yell?" Taek grimaces and walks over to Jeffrey. His words sound as tense as the lips drawn across his teeth. "Next time," he utters, "please knock! Sami's in his bedroom." Jeffrey runs by, leaving streaks of grime across the new carpet. "*Jeffrey! Your shoes!*" Since Jeffrey heard no order for action, he merely gives Taek a look befitting the utterance of any verbless noun—which is to say, Jeffrey's shoes stay on. All his reserve now exhausted, Taek booms, "*Take them off!*" Olivia flashes Taek a look of censure, and he shrugs an apology in his wife's direction.

Jeffrey looks puzzled but unruffled as he responds, "Oh. Ok." He sits down in the hallway and takes off his mud-caked shoes, ceremoniously laying them on the carpet. Taek simmers as he picks up the shoes and puts them outside the door.

Olivia places a comforting hand on Taek's shoulder and laughingly teases her husband. "Well, darling, I hate to leave just after our company arrives, but I'll be late if I don't get going." She walks out into the garage only to confront Jeffrey's bike parked right behind her car. She huffily grabs the handlebars and shoves it out of the way, out onto the driveway.

Inside the house, things aren't going much better. The boys' mad game of chase nearly knocks Taek off his (unshod) feet, which at the time were pointed toward the refrigerator to see what remained of the boys' snack raid. As he rights himself, he yells, "Hey, *guys*! Take the roughhousing outside!"

By the time Olivia returns, Taek is desperate. "Olivia," he pleads, "make up some kind of excuse and send the kid home!"

"Why?" she she says with a laugh. "Jeffrey hasn't even broken anything yet!" When Taek drills her with a knowing look that tells her the event is probably imminent, she says, "I'll take a plate of cookies over to Jeffrey's parents and welcome them to the neighborhood." After a pause for effect and perhaps the fun of seeing her husband's pained expression, she adds, " . . . and I'll take the boys with me."

A few minutes later, as Olivia raises her hand to knock on her new neighbors' door, Jeffrey announces, "You can go in." He opens the door and yells, "Mom!" Olivia hesitates at the doorway and politely knocks on the jamb. Jeffrey's mother, Debbie, appears and welcomes Olivia with a friendly wave.

"Come on *in*!" she says. "I'm so used to our old neighbors wandering right in that, when I heard you knock, I thought you might be a door-to-door salesperson!" She glances out the door before she closes it and says to her son, "Jeffrey! Put your bike in the garage. You *know* it doesn't belong in the driveway."

Olivia mentally notes the two families' differing rules as she bends down to remove her shoes. Debbie waves the gesture away in a friendly tone. "Oh, you don't need to do that." Quickly surveying the set, Olivia sees that Debbie and Jeffrey are wearing their shoes, and their home's hardwood floors aren't much affected by the dirt.

Olivia and Debbie sit down at the kitchen table to snack on the cookies. Olivia turns to see Jeffrey and Sami rooting through the refrigerator for something to drink. Olivia is relieved when Debbie turns toward Jeffrey, thinking perhaps that she is about to enforce what is surely a universal household rule—kids shouldn't be digging around in the refrigerator without permission. But Debbie is taking a different direction. "Jeffrey, could you bring us some pop, too, honey?" she chirps.

Just then, Jeffrey's father comes in through the front door, yelling as he arrives, "Hey, Jeffrey! Where are ya?" As Jeffrey and Sami race to the entryway, Olivia cringes at the stamping of running feet and *three* loud voices—the boys screeching and Jeffrey's dad roaring as they pretend he is a monster giving chase.

The Hidden Message

"When at our house, we expect you to abide by our rules—and we assume you know what those rules are by some strange psychic osmosis."

Think About It

Jeffrey isn't a bad kid; he merely has been raised under different rules. Our family history, cultures, personalities—even specific family decisions—govern our notions of proper behavior. They color our perceptions of others' actions and attitudes. This story about Jeffrey and Sami demonstrates how two different but equally functional families can have two vastly different sets of rules.

Changes You Can Make

Whenever you negatively judge the behavior of someone else's child, stop and ask yourself if what you are seeing is indeed misbehavior. The child may well be learning, and operating with, a different set of values from those of your family. As in so many other life situations, "different" does not necessarily mean "bad" or "wrong." In any case, unless you intend to raise your child as a hermit, you will have other people's children in your home from time to time who will not know your rules, or who will know them but break them nonetheless. You'll probably have to correct these children eventually, if only to keep your peace of mind. The easiest way to do this is to state your rule politely and clearly. As an example, when Jeffrey enters the house without knocking, Taek can say, "Jeffrey, when you come to our house, please knock or ring the bell and wait for someone to let you in." If this rule differs greatly from his life experience, Jeffrey will need a few repetitions to absorb it. The good news is that children are remarkably resilient; they can and do learn rules for different situations in record time.

Sometimes, your efforts to curb the behavior will fail. You then have several options. First, decide if (1) the behavior is just an annoyance or (2) the behavior is borne of another other family's rule system (or lack thereof) that you find unacceptable.

If the behavior gets under your skin but causes no other harm, ignore it; don't waste energy trying to change another family's way of life. That would be futile and presumptuous. Just repeat this mantra when you find yourself getting irritated: "It's not my kid, it's not my problem!"

If, however, you can't ignore the behavior—and it really is misbehavior and not the product of differing lifestyles—you can take the initiative to minimize it under your roof. Try monitoring the children's time together. Plan games or activities that require concerted attention, thus leaving less time for unstructured and undisciplined behavior. Or make a deal of sorts with the offending child. Tell him that here, in your house, you have certain rules, and the child is welcome to play here as long as he follows them, and if he doesn't, you'll have to ask him to leave. He will then be forced to either decide that he doesn't like your rules and will play elsewhere, or abide by your rules in exchange for your child's company.

If you've tried to make these changes on your own but aren't successful in gaining the child's cooperation, you may choose to talk with the child's parents. Sometimes, by letting them know what practices are important to you, you can enlist their efforts in encouraging their child to abide by your rules when visiting your home. Certainly, if the child's behavior endangers people, pets, or property, a polite but honest word with the parents is in order.

4

Messages About Relationships

The Referee Effect

It was the kind of task best done with a partner, and Ron and Noelle were good at working together. They were combining their efforts to put together a new bookshelf unit for their family room. As they consulted the cryptic instructions and deciphered which piece fit where, they were relieved that their two children were quietly and happily playing together in another room. The bookshelf eventually would house the children's books and be an attractive addition to the decor, but first, there was the challenge of assembly, which was obviously going to take the better part of the afternoon.

Or maybe longer . . . , thought Noelle when she heard a squabble upstairs. Resigned, she handed the instructions to Ron with her eyes rolled heavenward and said, "You'd think that at eight and ten years old, the kids could play together for a few minutes without fighting!" She pulled off her work gloves and headed toward the door, muttering, "I'll handle it." Upstairs, she found Joey and Kathy fighting over the building blocks from which they routinely created their architectural masterpieces. From the doorway, with her hands on her hips, she barked, "Ok, what's happening?"

Each child's voice battled the other to be heard first. "He's taking all the best pieces!" shrieked Kathy.

"Am not!" Joey retorted. "Just look at her pile over there! You'd think she was building the Empire State Building! She's the one taking all the best pieces!"

"You're a liar," snarled Kathy.

"And you're a jerk," mumbled Joey.

"Hey! Knock off the name-calling!" interjected Noelle, her voice straining to prevail over theirs. She took a few minutes to divide the blocks evenly, and with a backward glance of warning, she went back downstairs, where Ron had made some good progress on the bookshelf. The back section stood straight and even, corners nicely dovetailed and sharp, but Ron had reached an impasse: where were the white connectors to which the instructions kept referring? The parents decided that the best strategy was to sort the hardware, before any got lost. They hadn't even moved on to the second set of doodads before they heard Kathy yelling at the top of her lungs.

"Mommeeeeeee! Joey's taking my blocks!" Noelle handed a pile of—what were these things?—to Ron and again took flight upstairs. She redistributed the building blocks and tried to convince the kids to share nicely. With a hope that they'd do as they were told, she made her exit.

Once back on the assembly job, Noelle held up shelves as Ron secured them to the framework with the now organized hardware. One, two, three shelves were put in place, and the bookshelf was taking shape. Pleased, Noelle mused to Ron, "It's sure pleasant when the kids are quiet and happy." More shouts from the peanut gallery quickly reminded her, however, that wise parents never jinx themselves. Noelle closed her eyes. "I'll get it this time," said Ron.

Ron marched into the kids' room and, thinking maybe Noelle had been a little easy on them, announced his arrival in a loud, authoritative voice. "Enough! Put the blocks away and find something else to do!" He stayed just long enough to see that the kids followed his instructions, then returned to his own task. As he rejoined Noelle, he joked that at least *they* knew how to share their building materials!

Finally, the bookshelf was complete. Ron and Noelle collapsed into kitchen chairs with tall glasses of lemonade, complimenting each other on a job well done. Their respite was short lived, however, as Kathy and Joey's voices intruded upon the tranquil moment. This time, they were competing for possession of the TV remote. Again, Ron took over, snatching the remote from the kids, shutting off the TV, and ushering them outside to play.

The Hidden Message

"If you want our attention, all you have to do is yell and fight. One of us will be right there to solve the problem for you."

Think About It

When parents allow their children to drag them into every argument, everyone in the family suffers. The parents become frustrated from the constant pressure to act as referee and solve every dispute; the children become sullen and resentful toward each other and toward their parents, keeping score of every nuance that could indicate bias. Furthermore, by becoming involved in every argument, parents actually teach their children to fight louder and longer. The kids come to see their fights' increasing volume and duration as the call for help that will bring a parent to the room swiftly, ready to settle the problem and dispense attention.

And in the ensuing melee, each child will *compete* for that attention, seizing the opportunity to sway the parent over to his or her side and away from the opposing sibling. The parent's willing intervention conveniently presents the possibility of winning a battle in the endless war over possessions, time, space, and parental affection. It puts all the focus on the parent, instead of the source of dispute. Consider what would have happened if Noelle had compounded the problem by taking sides—what if she had said, "Yes, Joey [or Kathy], you're absolutely right. You get all the blocks now." Do you think the victorious child would continue playing with the blocks? No; more likely, he or she would leave the room with Mom—tossing a smug, gloating smile at the other sibling.

Moreover, if parents intercede and give their children attention *only* when they are fighting, and ignore them when they are getting along, the children subconsciously learn that the only way to capture their parents' attention is to argue and fight.

The "referee effect" deprives the children of the opportunity to learn the arts of negotiation and compromise—skills they will need throughout life. The family home is the first proving ground, where children must learn to live with others, even in the midst of disagreement. Their success or failure here extends beyond the childhood relationship. Siblings who never learn to understand each other inevitably grow up to be siblings who lose touch, or maintain a social acquaintance that lacks emotional depth. On the other hand, siblings who do learn to communicate with each other in times of disagreement also tend to communicate in times of pleasure, and often grow into adults with a close, loving, and supportive relationship.

Changes You Can Make

I have one piece of advice when it comes to interfering in your children's fights: Teach your children the skills *they* need to deal with each other—and then step out of the picture.

Wouldn't it be easy if that were all I had to say, and if the solution were as straightforward as that? There are several circumstances to consider, however, before you can completely take yourself out of your children's spats. If your children are young, or if they have come to rely on your skills of arbitration, they will need some guidance and training before you back out of the scene. Following my advice will be much easier and more rewarding after you teach your children the skill—and the pleasure—of negotiating and compromising with each other.

Noelle's and Ron's handling of their children's disputes demonstrates the absolute worst way to involve yourself in your children's squabbles. What they did each time was to solve the problem. Whether a polite distribution of blocks or a snatching away of the remote control, the result is the same: nobody gains anything positive. The parent takes control, and the children blindly concede. They have learned nothing . . . which means that the same situation will occur over and over again.

A better solution is to treat each squabble as an excellent opportunity to teach your children important life skills. (See! Now you can hardly wait for the next "golden opportunity.")

Let's say your children are arguing over the remote control and which TV program to watch. This is a perfect time to get involved *in the right way*. Quietly, and with emotions in rein, walk into the room. Gently turn off the television. Take the remote control and place it on the table. Ask, tell, or command your children to sit on the sofa side by side. Inform them that they may turn on the TV once they "have a plan." If you've so firmly placed yourself in the position of referee that you even wear a whistle around your neck, you may find your children being quiet purely from the shock of your new approach!

Take advantage of the moment to explain that they must discuss the issue and come to a mutually acceptable solution. You might even make a few suggestions: "You guys could check the TV guide and each agree to a specific show for today, or you may decide to split up and have one person watch the TV in the family room. Or perhaps you'll decide to keep the TV off and find something else to do right now."

Follow this up with a belief statement: "I believe in the two of you. You guys are capable of coming up with a good solution." If the kids seem at a loss as to how to begin, you may want to stay and "mediate"—which means only that you will guide their conversation. If at any time one of them begins to talk to *you*, make certain that you interrupt and say, "This is between you and your sister. I'd like you to talk to *her*."

Stay with them until they get the hang of it and actually begin to negotiate and discuss possible solutions, and to arrive at one they both agree will work. Follow this same procedure with each session of bickering that occurs between the two of them. I promise that you will begin to hear them following this pattern of their own accord, without your continued guidance, because, with training, they will eventually learn the important life skills of conflict resolution, compromise, and negotiation.

Does that seem like too much work? True, it's much quicker to grab the remote and send them outside to play. But to do what? Begin another squabble over another topic, and so on, ad nauseam, until one or both of them grow up and leave the house? You don't want that—and truth be told, neither do they. So, decide now what is *really* too much work.

(A word of caution here: If you have children who engage in frequent intense battles, it would be wise to seek the advice of a family counselor or therapist. Do not leave children who are physically fighting alone; that *is* the time for you to step between them. This section addresses the typical verbal bickering that goes on between siblings.)

The New Baby

Barbara and Anwar are proud and happy: today, they're bringing home Emma—a brand-new baby sister for Claire. Soon, for the very first time, Claire will look into the eyes of her baby sister, of whom she'll surely become passionately enamored. At just three years apart in age, the girls are bound to become friends and playmates in no time at all, and the very first moment of their lifelong bond is just a doorknob's twist away. The rush of emotion that so often accompanies parents through pregnancy and the postpartum phase threatens to overwhelm the well-meaning parents as they approach the front door.

Barbara's mother greets tiny new Emma at the threshold with the same happy tears and open arms that seem to greet the baby everywhere on these, her first days. Although she's already seen the tiny cherub at the hospital, Grandma can't resist plucking her out of Barbara's hands for a cuddle and coo. A while passes before Grandma hears quick breaths behind her and feels the plaintive stare of a wary child. She turns to see Claire peering around the corner, eyes huge in her tiny face. "Come see your new sister," Grandma chirps.

As Claire makes her way to the baby, Grandma peels back the blanket to reveal a tiny, red . . . something. What is *this*? Claire thinks. She knew the baby wouldn't be born as a big three-year-old like herself, but she's never seen anything quite like this! A wrinkly, bleary-eyed raisin of a sister, a fascinating, blinking, breathing being currently regarding her big sister with the searching eyes unique to infants. A brand-new people, she thinks. Emma. My *little sisser*. Emma. She rolls the baby's name over her tongue, liking the sensation. "This kid's gonna love me, I'd better start teaching her stuff right away, so we can play . . ." she says, half to herself and half out loud.

As her peanut-butter-covered fingers reach out to the baby's face for a preschool-style welcome, Grandma intercedes. "Ohhh. *Careful*, honey. We don't want to get the baby all dirty. And your hands, they might have germs . . ." Claire sheepishly pushes her sticky hands into her pockets; she should have known that, she guesses. Shouldn't she? She leans over to study her baby sister, the wonder of it all apparent in her eager face.

"Hi, little sisser," Claire tentatively says, "I'm your big. . . ah . . . ah-*choo*!"

Grandma sweeps the baby away, and Mommy appears with a tissue. "Oh, dear, you have to be careful not to sneeze on the baby."

"Oκ," Claire absently answers. "Mommy, can we go to the park?"

Barbara hugs her big girl and tells her, "Maybe later, honey. Right now, Mommy has to feed the baby."

As Barbara settles in on the sofa and her cherished task of breast-feeding, Claire climbs up next to her, favorite book in hand. "Mommy read to me?" Claire asks as she hands the book over to her, looking for her free hand but finding both filled with Emma.

"Not now, honey. The baby is just learning how to do this, and I need to concentrate." Barbara shifts in her seat, seeking the best position for her and the baby. Claire gets out of the chair, sensing that she's in the way. She stands a safe distance away, wondering what Mommy's milk tastes like—she can't seem to remember—and imagining her mother's soft arms around her.

As the baby falls into a blissful postnursing sleep, Barbara lays her in the pretty new cradle. Not a minute later, Claire comes roaring through the room with her new plastic airplane, one she's sure will delight her little sister. Barbara's soft but swift admonishment grounds the action in mid-flight. "Shhhh! Don't wake the baby, sweetheart."

Claire drops her airplane and peeks into the cradle. Those eyelids—they look almost transparent! She's just reaching in to touch them, and all those other body parts so fascinating in their newness, when Anwar rushes over. "No, *no*, Claire. Don't touch the baby's eyes. Uh . . . why don't I read to you?" He shows her a new book he picked up in the hospital gift shop, appropriately titled *A New Baby in Joey's House.* As Anwar settles into the chair with Claire, he tells her how lucky she is to have a new baby sister to play with. Claire, reserved without knowing quite why, looks forward to hearing if Joey can actually *play* with *his* baby sister.

The Hidden Message

"The new baby is a special, fragile, precious person—much more important to us than you are. From now on, everything you say or do will be affected by her presence. From now on, she comes first."

Think About It

The whole postpartum scenario produces a confusing whirl of emotions that envelops everyone in the household in those first tender weeks. In our instinctive drive to keep newborns from harm, we often become overzealous. Thus, we protect the baby but not her sibling's feelings, driving a wedge between the children from the very beginning. The words and actions we use to shield our infants inadvertently seem defensive, accusatory, and negative to our older children, who often do not, or cannot, communicate the hurt. If they are beyond two or three years in age, siblings may perceive that they should be happy at such a time and become perplexed as to why they feel sad.

When we brought home our newest baby, Coleton, our son, David, was already a bright and talkative seven-year-old, young enough to feel the impact of this newcomer but also old enough to voice his concerns. A few days after we came home from the hospital, David and I were eating breakfast together. Coleton was in his typical place—my arms. David, who'd been unusually quiet, suddenly glanced at me and shook his head, saying, "Already it's the baby, the baby, the baby. If I want a hug, I can give you one, but you can't give me one." (If you're curious—I then put Coleton in his cradle and took David over to the sofa for a morning snuggle, reassuring him that we could do that whenever he needed a hug.)

All the confusion an older sibling is feeling, coupled with the unintended negativity from parents, can discourage siblings from getting to know the newcomer and may sow the seeds for the dreaded "sibling rivalry." It may also drive our older children to act out in ways that we see as "naughty" but are desperate pleas for attention and equal billing.

Changes You Can Make

As with many situations in parenting, awareness of the hidden message can eliminate much of the problem. If you are living this scenario, you are probably gasping in the surprise of recognition—and if you have lived through this life stage, you are now sagging at the memory.

In addition to becoming more aware of the implications of your actions, some very simple strategies can promote a positive experience for your older child (or children) when a new baby enters the family. First and foremost, acknowledge that this is a time of adjustment for everyone—time to reduce your outside activities, relax your housekeeping standards, and focus on your current priorities: adapting to your new family size and paving the way for healthy sibling relationships. I know that this is a tall order. But babies are babies for such a short period that it's worth it to allow yourself this time to build a foundation for the future.

And just how do you foster sibling friendship from the beginning? One way is to understand and validate your older child's feelings. Things *have* changed, and not just for you. The next time you're holding the new baby, take a moment to look at an older sibling while he or she is unaware of your gaze; you might just catch a glimpse through the window of your child's eye. Like you, your older child may be more tired than usual, a little more stressed, a little touchier. It's a natural reaction. The baby does require much time and attention, and will continue to dominate and disrupt family life for a while. Be sure to let your older children know you're aware that they're struggling with this concept—and that that it's OK. Statements like "I know it's hard to wait for Emma to wake up until we go to the park" will help your children hear that you care about their feelings.

Avoid blaming everything on "the baby"—a common error. This story demonstrates some of the creative ways we do exactly that. "Don't get *the baby* dirty." "Be careful not to sneeze on *the baby*." "We can't go now; Mommy has to feed *the baby*." "Don't wake *the baby*." "Don't touch *the baby*." Very soon, your older child will be ready to send *the baby* back to whence it came! Of course, "the baby" really is the reason for all of your schedule changes, and for the required behavior changes from your child, but it behooves you to watch your wording. A few multipurpose statements for schedule changes include "My hands are busy right now," "We'll go later, after lunch/nap/TV show," "Yes, we will, in about twenty minutes," and "Not right now."

When addressing the behavior changes that you require of your child, make the subject of your comment the activity itself instead of its connection to "the baby." "Your hands are dirty; let's go wash them." "Remember to cover your mouth when you sneeze."

Accept your child's curiosity about the new baby, whom she will want to touch and hold. Allow your child to explore, hold, and feel the baby when the baby is asleep. Once your child is a bit more experienced (and the baby a bit sturdier), let your child hold and caress the awake, alert baby. And encourage your child to touch and talk to the baby when the little one is safe in your arms. Touch and communication are important to *both* of them and to their budding relationship. You and your older child will soon be rewarded and delighted by smiles of recognition from the little one.

If you are breast-feeding, an older child who has been weaned may exhibit fascination with your breast milk. Consider letting her have a taste (on a spoon or in a cup, if you're more comfortable with that) so she doesn't feel excluded from some mysterious ritual or culinary treat. It certainly won't hurt her, and one taste will be enough to convince her that she *much* prefers her 'big girl' glass of chocolate milk.

Use positive terms to patiently teach your older child how to touch and play with the baby. Avoid using "no," and replace it with affirmative instructions. As an example, instead of saying, "No! Don't touch the baby's eyes," you can say, "Emma's eyes are very delicate; touch her instead on her cheeks and her chin." You can also use the baby herself to teach your child; your child will be amused as you play ventriloquist, putting words in the baby's mouth. "I like when you smile at me!" for example, or "I'll stay nice and clean if you wash your hands before we play."

Avoid overusing "no" and "stop" by mastering an approach I call "hover and rescue." Hover over your children, and intervene only if you see the activity straying from your comfort zone. If it does, pick the baby up, distract the older child, and move on to something else. When our third child, David, was born—his sisters were two and four—this was a lifesaving technique on which I often relied.

Give your older child practical information about babies— that they sleep a lot, nurse a lot, have a noisy and loud cry, and will have lots of messy diapers, and that it will be a while before the baby turns into a fun playmate. Teach the older sibling how to be helpful with the baby, without expecting your firstborn to become a built-in baby-sitter. Encourage and praise whenever things are going right. Help your child take delight in the ways she's earning the title "big sister."

It's a great occasion to pull out photos and movies of your older child as a baby. As you go through them, help your child see that not so long ago, she was the baby who was getting special attention.

The new baby will require extensive care and commitment from you. But make sure that your older child is also getting some one-on-one Mommy/Daddy/Grandma/caregiver interaction. Allowing time for a shared game, book, or cuddle can go a long way toward helping your older child feel secure in your love for her.

Above all, *talk*. Encourage your child to vent feelings, good and bad; let your child know that these feelings are natural, so that she doesn't feel "bad." Ask her what she thinks, and listen without judgment. Commiserate with your child, and reassure her that this phase will pass, that things will seem more "normal" soon, and that the baby eventually will become a child who will talk, play, and run with her. Read together some of the many books available for children that depict the conflicts faced by an older child when a new baby enters the family. It will be reassuring to your child to learn that other big brothers and sisters have the same mixed feelings about their new sibling.

Our baby, Coleton, is now four months old, and our family has settled nicely into its new configuration. Just yesterday I asked ten-year-old Vanessa if having a baby in the house is different than she expected it would be. "Yes," she answered, "I didn't know he would make everybody so happy." David adores his baby brother, too, which is evident by the many hugs he showers him with. And Coleton, well, he thinks his big sisters and brother hung the moon.

With a little heart, increased awareness, and a few new tactics, you can enjoy this remarkable transformation in your family.

Father and Son

Charles sat at his desk, head in his hands, heart in his throat—and all of him in the fog that shrouded his life since the shock of his divorce. It was hard enough getting used to being single again; adapting to single fatherhood went beyond his notions of challenge. Parenting with a partner was so much easier. Today, nothing seemed clear. Nothing, that is, except his love for his son. Tim was a good kid who gave him little trouble beyond typical boyhood mischief. The child was his father's beacon in this new and uncertain sea of singlehood. "Well," Charles said aloud but only to himself, "enough worry. We're gonna be just fine." He sounded surer than he felt. He watched the hands of the clock tick round until they read 3:45. "Thank God," he said to the walls. "Time to pick Tim up."

As he pulled the car up in front of the elementary school, he spotted Tim chatting with friends in front of the flagpole. Charles pushed open the door. "Hiya, bud! Hop in!" Tim said his good-byes and climbed into the car. Charles reached over and gave his son a hug. "What should we do for dinner? Grocery store or fast food?"

Tim pondered a minute. "I got lots of homework tonight," he said. "What's quicker?"

"Hmmm. It's probably a wash, depending on what we eat. We could stop on the way home and grab a burger, or we could pick up some stuff at the store, and I'll cook while you start on your homework. What do you think?"

Tim scrunched up his face in thought. "Let's just grab a burger."

Charles nodded. "Burgers it is."

The twosome stopped at the local fast-food restaurant and ordered some eats from the drive-through. Charles wished his son had gone for the salad he'd suggested in addition to the fries and burgers, but it had been a long, hard day, and he wanted to just enjoy Tim's company. On the way home, between bites, they exchanged stories of their days. Tim told his dad about the weird substitute teacher that they had to live through. Charles had Tim laughing with stories of a confused coworker who continually put documents in the copier face up and in the fax machine face down. All of the hapless coworker's copies and faxes came out blank. Tim always got a kick out of the stories his dad recounted about his workday; he almost felt as if he knew the people.

As they pulled up to their home, Tim spotted his friend Garrison on his bike across the street. "Dad," he requested, "would you take my backpack in the house? I'm gonna go ride with Garrison."

"But Tim," Charles answered, "I thought you had lots of homework tonight?"

"Yeah, but I can do it later."

"Well, OK, but not too long, then. Why don't I call you in about an hour?"

Tim was already out of the car and boarding his bike. "*Daaad!* Two hours at the least!"

"OK. Two hours, but not a minute later. And put your helmet on."

"Dad, *nobody* wears helmets anymore," Tim protested, his voice trailing behind him as he set off, eager to catch up with his friend.

"They do so!" Charles responded. "All the professionals and serious bike riders do. It's just the goofy kids who don't."

Tim rolled his eyes. "I'm just gonna be on our street!" He was barely within earshot now.

"Tim!" yelled Charles, "*helmet*!"

But Tim was already gone.

With a sigh, Charles began cleaning the fast-food debris out of the car. He threw a quick wave toward his neighbor, Karen, as she was walking up her driveway. After they exchanged pleasantries across the lawn, Karen (well known for being a protective mother) mentioned that Tim should really be wearing his helmet. Charles leaped to Tim's defense. "Oh, he's just going to be on our street—and only for a short while."

Two hours later, Charles stepped out the front door and called for Tim, who appeared shortly. "Two hours are up. Come on in and start your homework."

"Aww, Dad," complained Tim, "Garrison's parents let him stay out 'til 8:00, and he has plenty of time to do his homework."

"Are you sure that will give you enough time?" Charles prodded.

"Yeah, Dad, honest."

"OK, then, 8:00. And not a minute later."

Just after 8:00, Tim bounded through the door. He grabbed his backpack and a snack and plunked down at the kitchen table.

A while later, Charles proclaimed it time for a shower. Tim's response was that he had taken a shower *Monday* night, and besides, he still had homework. Charles shook his head, mumbled "OK," and plodded into his office. Charles became so entrenched in his work that he didn't even look up until after 9:30. He pushed away from his desk and entered the kitchen, where he found Tim, surrounded by chips and pop cans, still working on his homework.

"Tim! It's past your bedtime!"

"Yeah, Dad, I know, but I'm almost done."

Charles scanned Tim's assorted papers. "What have you got left to do?" He sat down next to Tim and helped him finish the last of his assignment.

The Hidden Message

"You and me—we're buddies. Kinda like roommates."

Think About It

Your child should have friends—but he should find them at school and at the playground. At home, he should find a parent, a caregiver in charge on whom he can rely for sound direction, consistent rules, and loving support. "Friends" negotiate joint decisions, mull over the possibilities, and give each other suggestions, but a friend respects his friend's right to his own decisions. A "parent," on the other hand, sets boundaries, creates rules, and—whether the child is happy about it or not—enforces those rules.

Parents fall into this "friendship trap" for a variety of reasons. One, as this story demonstrates, is a sort of codependency that sometimes occurs after a divorce or a spouse's death. The parent finds himself struggling with his own lot in life and turns to his child for friendship, companionship, and validation. The parent's feelings of guilt and sadness for breaking up the child's home plus the overwhelming pressure of being both Mom and Dad often equal a tendency to overindulge the child.

Parents also ensnare themselves in the friendship trap because they're human: when we feel vulnerable, sometimes we need to feel love and acceptance, and we take inappropriate actions to gain them. The pattern is often set in toddlerhood, when a parent gives a child a forbidden cookie because it's easier than contending with a pint-size temper tantrum. Yet another reason that parents fail to step into their role as leader is a distrust of authority and a reluctance to appear too firm or stodgy. And some are just too weary or apathetic to put forth the effort to discipline their children.

However it's created, the problem is that, as in so many other situations, we are not as strong or effectual when we come to an emotional situation out of need. And whatever the reason, the result is the same: the child is left to flounder through childhood without a life jacket.

Changes You Can Make

What do you think is your most important job in raising your children? To answer that question, perhaps it is more helpful to consider what it is *not*. It is *not* to make them happy with you. It is *not* to convince them what a wonderful person you are. It is *not* to gain their undying affection. Rather, your overriding duty is to raise capable, responsible young people who, when mature, will stand on their own, sure of themselves and their values. To attain this goal, you need to set limits, create rules, and impose consequences; therefore, you must accept that your child will be unhappy, angry, or annoyed with you occasionally. (And sometimes, often.)

I'm not suggesting that you become emotionally blind to your children's feelings. It's essential to be aware of those feelings. I am asking you to realize that it's much kinder in the long run to help them learn what they need to know now, at your apron strings, rather than at the mercy of the world at large. When we respectfully, lovingly, but firmly impose proper boundaries on our children, when we give them guidance and discipline, we will help them to develop their own *inner* discipline as they grow up. It's that inner strength that will keep them standing in even the worst of life's storms. And it's what will allow them to reach toward their own happiness, unfettered by insecurities and doubt.

Your child will have many friends in his life, and he will certainly enjoy them. He may even learn important life lessons from friends. But friends come and go, and some of the lessons are not necessarily ones you want your child to learn. On the other hand, a nurturing parent who provides guidance and direction, with no hidden agendas and with nothing but the child's well-being in mind, earns a love and respect that will last forever. A strong parent teaches the central lessons, morals, and values that shape a child's future. You can serve your child best, and show your love most, by taking on the role of parent with confidence and leadership. Then, one day, you'll look eye-to-eye with an adult, whom you still call "child" but whom you can also—finally and appropriately—call "friend."

A Parent's Work Is Never Done

Jean awoke to the delightful sensation of her husband rubbing her back. "Ummmm," she murmured; it felt good. Ray continued for a time, then moved his hands around to the front of her body. Jean playfully slapped them away. "Stop! It's a school day. We need to get the kids up pretty soon!" Ray didn't take the hint and continued his amorous advances. Jean giggled and rolled off the edge of the bed. "You behave!" she teased as she went into the bathroom to shower and dress.

Ray was still snoozing under the covers when Jean was done in the bathroom. She sat on the edge of the bed and kissed the lump she most suspected was his head. "Come on, sleepyhead. Time to get up. I'm going to wake the boys."

Ray finally crawled out of bed, as Jean bustled about the house waking the boys, putting together lunches, and signing permission slips. Ray padded about, too, making breakfast and throwing laundry into the machine.

Jean and Ray ran a successful desktop publishing business from their home. The phone never seemed to stop ringing, and today was no exception. The phone's jangle and the whir of fax transmissions punctuated their morning routine, the tempo of which was heating up. Soon, they were moving so fast that only the whoosh of air as one passed the other reminded them of their shared presence.

As soon as their boys, Blake and Chris, got dressed and finished breakfast, they began digging through the box of last year's

Halloween costumes and supplies. "Mom!" Blake called, "I want to be an alien again, but I can't find any rubber gloves for alien hands. Could you please get some for me?"

"Sure," Jean answered. "I'll pick some up on the way back from my meetings today."

Chris heard this and added his own request. "I have to bring the treat to my soccer game Saturday. Can you get some granola bars—peanut butter ones—and juice?"

"Will do," Jean answered as she added those items to her grocery list. Ray sneaked up behind her and whispered his own request in her ear. "Ray!" she whispered, as a blush crept up her cheeks, "Shhh. The boys might hear you!"

Just then, a fearsome clamor arose from the laundry room. Jean and Ray looked up with the same mixture of startle and dread. Arriving in the laundry room, they watched the machine dance about, leaking a little from the bottom. "I'll take care of it," Ray said, and set about determining the machine's current problem.

Before long, the boys were out the door, and their parents went about their morning routine. Jean put the remains of the Halloween supplies back into the box as she fielded phone calls, hoping her clients didn't sense her multitasking.

One call, however, was casual, and Jean welcomed a few moments of catching up with her friend, Donna. After covering their own goings-on, they moved along to kid updates and car pool schedules, then Donna took the conversation in another direction. "A bunch of us are going to start a bowling team! I know we haven't bowled since high school, but Arrow Lanes has a special couples league on Tuesday nights. It's not real competitive, and it sounds like fun. They even serve pizza and stuff, so dinner's part of the package. Think you and Ray could do it?"

Jean thought for a minute. "Did you say Tuesday nights? When does it start?" Donna checked the schedule and noted that the new season began in two weeks. "Oh, that's too bad," said Jean, "Both of the boys have soccer practice on Tuesday. I guess we'll have to pass. But thanks for the invite."

"You're welcome. Maybe next time," Donna suggested. They finished up their conversation, exchanging soccer team stories and Halloween plans. Jean hung up the phone, wondering if she liked bowling and a little amazed that she didn't remember.

Ray emerged from the laundry room. "The thing was just a little off balance, hon. But that leak is back even more than ever . . . maybe I ought to go shop for a new machine." He went down to the office to check the phone book for appliance dealers but inevitably got sucked into the black hole of unfinished and pending assignments.

The phone rang again. Blake, from school, nearly cried into the receiver. "Mom, our field trip is after lunch, and I forgot my permission slip!"

"Oh, Blake," Jean droned. "I signed it this morning—what'd you do with it?" After an on-the-spot search, she answered her own question. "Here it is on the counter. I'm just about to leave. I'll drop it off before my meetings, on my way to the printer's."

As she hung up, Ray called to her from the downstairs office. "Hon? Are you planning to be home when the boys arrive from school, or shall I? Who's got what tonight? Isn't tonight soccer and Boy Scouts? Is this the night we have that conflict? I'll do the Boy Scout run; you take soccer . . ."

"That's fine," Jean mumbled. The dog sniffed at her feet and plunked himself down, a scrap of paper hanging from his jowls. "What the . . ." She gasped when she saw the library book about ten feet behind the dog—a book with a few teeth marks. She could add the cost of *that* book to the late fee for those reference books she borrowed a few weeks ago that were now overdue.

Jean began to see her day shaping up as an errand-fest that required a written reminder list, lest she forget something. She quickly wrote one up and shut the list in her portfolio, along with the grocery list—and the signed permission slip—and barreled out the door. Just as she was about to shut it behind her, a thought hit her. Rushing back to the kitchen, she craned her neck around the corner. "Hey, I've got a break between twelve and one today. How about we meet for lunch?"

"That would be nice," Ray answered, "but I'm all over the map this morning."

"Maybe we can squeeze something in later this week?" Jean asked.

"Yeah, maybe," Ray answered. Then he remembered one more detail of the already hectic day: "Come to think of it, wasn't I supposed to do something for the Boy Scout meeting tonight? Construct a longhouse or something?" Jean passed along the information and made a beeline for the door.

The day buzzed on, more demands and more interruptions interspersed with the routine tasks of dinner prep, cleanup, and so on, and so on, and so on. Late that night, Jean fell into bed. Ray followed, as soon as he'd completed the logo design due the following day. Jean, grateful to feel his presence, also felt the need for physical contact, confirmation of the partnership that existed beyond their business. She reached out in the way she knew her husband loved.

Ray sighed. "Love you honey—but I hope you understand. I'm really wiped out tonight." She did understand, all too well. They smiled, kissed quickly, and turned over; both were asleep within minutes.

The Hidden Message

"I'm a parent, a breadwinner, and a home manager. There's just no time left to be a spouse, too!"

(While this story features the marriage relationship, many other relationships also involve adults who have children, and these words of wisdom apply equally to them.)

Think About It

Too many parents fall into this pattern. We try so hard to hold all the loose ends of our world together that we forget to nurture the primary relationship in the family—the relationship between man and woman that goes beyond the roles of mother/father/care-taker/worker.

Whatever the role that derails our marital efforts—mother, father, breadwinner, volunteer, athlete—the effect is the same: in the shuffle that it produces in our day-to-day lives, we sometimes lose sight of who and what our partner is and what draws us to that person. In the short term, this failure prevents us from enjoying our relationship with our spouse and leaves a gap in our lives. Continued over time, it can be devastating to a marriage.

The irony is that the weeds we allow to overtake our little garden of interpersonal relationship can also choke out our capacity to parent effectively. A happy partnership is the most fertile ground for our kids' development. They feel secure and content when they know that Mom and Dad love each other, and when they understand that the relationship between Mom and Dad is important and valued. In addition, by observing that adult relationship, they begin to form their own understanding of what marriage is all about, and they'll use what they've learned when the time comes for them to manage their own relationships as adults.

A commitment to spending time nurturing the marriage needn't compromise children's needs. Quite the contrary: kids grow tall in the reflected sunshine of a strong bond between parents. They flourish in the warmth of a stable and happy family environment. When the partnership is strong, healthy, and vibrant, all family members benefit. That bond cannot hold with only minimal attention. At most, the partnership will merely survive; at worst, it will wither and die. A healthy, strong, loving union requires time, patience, attention, and care.

Changes You Can Make

You perform many functions; you have many roles. This multiplicity is what makes you who you are and what makes your life so rich. But don't allow any of these roles to overtake the one that underlies your mental, emotional, physical, and family health: your role as life partner.

To create or maintain a strong, stable marriage, you must begin with a commitment to put time, effort, and thought into nurturing your relationship with your significant other. Let the force of this commitment guide you in making good decisions.

Jean, for instance, could set the alarm just a few minutes earlier to welcome her husband's morning ideas. Ray could go to bed just a mite earlier to make time for his wife's affections. Both could block out the noon hour from client meetings and phone calls to enjoy lunch (or whatever activity they choose) together. They might look into carpooling to lessen the fatigue of running around delivering their children, or they could cut back on the kids' activities to spend more time together as a family. A sitter just once a week would allow them to join that bowling league, or perhaps try out different activities to reacquaint themselves with each other and relearn what they enjoy doing together. Jean and Ray could find time for a walk together by putting off grocery shopping for the next day—no one will starve in the meantime. But their relationship might.

A healthy marriage wouldn't require that they do all of these things, all the time. Even one or two minor revisions in a day could bring them closer together.

Another idea for strengthening your relationship is to weed the garden; strip away the noncritical and put the accent on the good in each other and in the relationship. Make it a habit to ignore the little annoyances—dirty socks on the floor, a day-old coffee cup on the counter, an inelegant burp at the dinner table— and choose instead to smell the roses.

And play nice. That may sound funny to you, but how many times do you see, or experience, partners treating each other in impolite, harsh ways that they'd never treat a friend? Sometimes we take our partners for granted and unintentionally display rudeness. As the saying goes, if you have a choice between being right and being nice, choose to be nice. Or to put this in the wise words of Bambi's friend Thumper (the bunny rabbit)—"If you can't say somethin' nice, don't say nothin' at all."

"Pick your battles." How often have you heard this advice in relation to parenting? This *is* great advice for child rearing—and it's great advice to follow in your marriage as well. In any human relationship there will be disagreement and conflict. The most productive mind-set here is to decide which bones are worth picking and which are better left alone. By doing this, you'll encounter much less negative energy between you.

Make touching and cuddling a priority. Usually, when couples first marry, this happens naturally. You can often identify newlyweds by their tendency to touch each other—holding hands, sitting close, touching arms, kissing—just as you can spot "oldlyweds" by how little they touch. Mothers of babies and young children often feel less need for physical contact with their partners; their little ones provide so much opportunity for touching and cuddling that day's end leaves them "touch fulfilled." So, here's a simple tip: Make it a point to touch your spouse more often. It doesn't take much—a pat, a hug, a shoulder massage—and the good feeling it produces for both of you far outreaches the effort.

Spend more time talking and listening to your partner. I don't mean, "Remember to pick up Jimmy's soccer uniform," or "I have a PTA meeting tonight." Rather, get into the habit of sharing your thoughts about what you read in the paper, what you watch on TV, your hopes, your dreams, your concerns. Take a special interest in the subjects in which your spouse is interested, and ask questions. And then listen to the answers.

And finally . . . spend time with your spouse. *Alone.* As adults. This doesn't mean you have to take a two-week vacation in Hawaii. (Although, that's fun too!) What's most important is to carve out small daily snippets when you can enjoy uninterrupted conversation, or even just quiet companionship, without a baby on your hip, a child tugging your shirtsleeve, or a teenager begging for the car keys. A daily morning walk around the block or a shared cup of tea after all the children are in bed will work wonders to reconnect you to each other.

When you and your spouse regularly connect in a way that nurtures your relationship, you may find a renewed love between you, as well as a refreshed vigor that will allow you to be a better, more loving parent. You owe it to yourself—and to your kids—to make your relationship strong.

Superwoman

Gina had just seen the kids off to school—another hectic but successful morning. She took a deep breath and thought about all the things she had to get done. The day's "to do" list was overwhelming, but she couldn't waste time fretting; she needed to get busy.

She rushed to her desk and called up the file for the article she'd *thought* was finished yesterday. Frustrated with her editor's penchant for last-minute changes, she pounded the keyboard just a little faster, just a little louder than usual, until she completed the revisions. She E-mailed the file and shut down the computer.

Next up was her daughter's costume for this evening's school play. Gina fished out her sewing supplies and began quickly pinning up the cape. Her haste earned her a good jab in the hand. Sucking on the end of her throbbing finger, she mumbled to herself, "If Erin had told me about this costume two weeks ago, I wouldn't be rushing through this!" Rush, though, she did, and the costume was finished in short order. She stashed it in a closet and wondered if she'd remember later where she'd put it. Then, in one smooth practiced motion, she whisked the keys off their hook, plucked up her purse, sashayed out the door, and slid into the car.

The first stop was the sports supply center. Her husband, Stuart, needed equipment to coach their son Nick's baseball team on the weekend that was fast approaching. She was only half sure that she'd picked the right items but in too much of a spin to agonize over it. As the ostensibly helpful salesclerk pelted Gina with questions that she was clueless to answer, she became annoyed. She grizzled silently: Stuart wants to manage this team; so why do I get stuck buying supplies I don't know anything about? The whole affair took much longer than she'd expected. She'd really have to hurry to get everything done before the kids came home from school.

Next on her route was a quick stop to pick up her mother's laundry. Already in a sour mood, she brushed off all her mother's attempts at pleasantries and instead asked in a rather clipped voice, "Do you think your washing machine will be repaired anytime in this *century*, Mom?" The ensuing hurt look produced enough guilt to warrant a short visit over a cup of coffee with her mother, who looked into her daughter's face and saw the signs of stress that only a mother can—at least for as long as Gina sat still. Her daughter's impatience was apparent with each frequent glance at the clock. Gina's cell phone rang just as she rose to leave.

"Honey, it's Stuart. I called the store, and they have one more thing for the baseball team up at the front desk. Could you stop by and pick it up?" Gina began to protest, but Stuart told her how much he appreciated the way she always helped him out. She swallowed her objection and promised to make the extra trip.

On her way back home from the store, Gina stopped at the school and checked her PTA mailbox. There was an urgent note from the head of the Bake Sale Committee: they were short on pies for tonight's play—could she manage to bring an extra? Gina raised her eyes to the heavens; this committee chairperson was so disorganized! She yanked a piece of paper out of her purse so roughly that she tore it in two. In bold black ink, she wrote "Pie" and mentally took stock of her pantry. She figured she had enough ingredients and went home to handle the Great Pie Crisis.

The flashing light on the answering machine greeted Gina's return. The first message elicited a groan. "Hi, Gina, it's Mark. I know I said I'd have the class outline done for our program, but something's come up." Not again! But true to form, her teaching partner went on with the latest excuse to shift his workload to her. ". . . So I E-mailed you the part I have done. Can you just finish it up before class on Monday?"

"Just what I need," Gina mumbled. "Another item for my never-ending list.

No sooner had she finished listening to her messages than the phone rang. Ann, mother of one of Erin's classmates, nearly burst with her greeting. "Gina! I'm so glad you're home! I just realized that the play starts at 7:30 tonight, but the girls need to be there at 7:00. My son's piano lesson isn't over until 7:15. I was wondering if you could possibly pick Katie up on your way over to school? I would really, really appreciate it."

"Sure, no problem," answered Gina, although what was going through her head was more like, "Yeah, right, Ann. You've always got some emergency that you've just happen to forget about until the very last minute. And then who do you call? Who does *everybody* call? Good old Gina."

Then the push was on. Gina cleared a work space in the kitchen and prepared the pie; while it baked, she warmed up leftover chicken to which she added a package of stuffing and some frozen peas. Gourmet it wasn't, but it would have to do. One of the kids didn't like last night's chicken, but she didn't have time to create a whole new meal.

Nearly breathless, she ticked off the last few items on her list just as the gang arrived home. The kids deposited their backpacks on the floor, and Stuart shrugged out of his coat. Someone asked the usual million-dollar question, "What's for dinner?" When Gina answered with the menu, she heard the three groans she knew she would.

"Oh, no, not *that* chicken," Nick griped.

That's all it took. Gina's face crumpled, and tears flowed down her cheeks. Sad as she looked, her overwhelming emotion was anger—which quickly became obvious. "*What am I?* Everyone's *servant*? I'm tired of taking care of everyone else. I do my best, and all I ever get are complaints. If you don't want chicken for dinner, then . . . then . . . make . . . your . . . own!" With that, she threw down her serving spoon and swept past them all into the bathroom for a good cry.

The (Not So) Hidden Message

"I'm a martyr. A miserable one. And it's all your fault. How can I possibly take care of everyone else when I don't take even a minute to take care of myself?"

Think About It

A ridiculous parody of a common situation as described in my book *Kid Cooperation* catches the essence of this message:

> *You have just boarded an airplane. A voice on the PA system narrates while the flight attendant demonstrates the use of the safety equipment on board the plane. As the attendant holds up the air mask, the voice says, "In the event of a loss of cabin pressure, an oxygen mask will drop from the ceiling above your seat. Pulling down on the air mask will begin the flow of air. Immediately assist your children with their masks. Then assist your spouse with his or her mask. After that, look behind you for any elderly or confused people, and help them with their masks. Double-check the people seated in the row across from you to be certain that their masks are secure. After following these steps, if you have any energy left, put a mask over your own face and gasp for air."*

As absurd as this sounds, many parents conduct their daily lives in just this way. They spend so much time and energy taking care of everyone and everything else around them that their "to do" list has no room left for their own needs. Giving is good, you say. So do I. But when things get to this point, this is not "giving." This is *taking*—taking on too much, taking over too

much, taking on guilt, and taking away the ene\
to be productive.

Neglecting your own emotional and physical n\
angry, resentful, and depressed—and with nothing\
give.

Changes You Can Make

To be a healthy, happy person, you must take good care of your-self. In doing so, you'll have more enthusiasm and energy to be able to take care of everyone else. To that end, your first, most important action is to acknowledge that taking care of yourself is not a selfish act. As a human being, with real emotional and phys-ical needs, you must feed your body, your mind, and your soul well to achieve the balance that enables you to care for the peo-ple and causes that you love.

So you've given yourself permission to add your own name to your "to do" list. What next? Here are a few ideas:

1. Learn to be a better time manager. When you're organized and efficient with your time, chances are you'll find more of it—enough for even yourself. Often, we rush about without a plan and waste vast chunks of our days. Orga-nizing a time management system will take some effort, but overall, it will make your days more orderly and you more productive. When you complement organization with specific daily routines (shopping on Mondays, clean-ing on Tuesdays . . .), you'll find your days flowing together in a pleasant, comfortable fashion.

2. Learn when to say yes and how to say no. Stop thinking that anytime anyone asks you to do anything you must say yes; when you automatically say yes when you'd like to say no, you feel put-upon, resentful, and angry, and your own goals are abandoned. Start making smart decisions about what you will or won't do. Amazing but true, if you don't

perform all those endless tasks, someone else will, if they're important enough. Of course, good manners are always essential, but there is a multitude of ways to say no while being polite and nice about it.

3. Relax your standards, and set your priorities. You can't be a parent, spouse, employee, volunteer, gourmet cook, house-keeper, and whatever else—and expect to do every job per-fectly and cheerfully. Instead, decide which ones require more time and attention, and which ones you can let slip by. *Choose* your priorities, instead of letting pressure from outside sources choose them for you.

4. Learn how to ask for what you want. This should be easy—employ the many techniques others have used on you! You'll be pleasantly surprised to see that people are often happy to help when the favor is reasonable and the request polite.

5. Take some time for yourself. Rediscover the tried-and-true pleasures that allow you to recharge your own battery, and schedule them in. You won't need a week at a private health spa to feel that you're taking care of yourself! Lunch with a friend, a cup of tea and a good novel, or a dance class a few times a week may be enough. When you take the time to take care of yourself, you revitalize your spirit, energize your body, and nourish your mind so that you *can* take care of everyone else's needs, and feel good about it.

5

Messages About Discipline and Behavior

Matt the Brat

Laila and her daughter Jennifer hopped out of their car, waving enthusiastically to fellow members of their weekly play group. Monica and her son Kevin, and Lisa and her daughter Kimmy had just pulled in; the van doors opened, and the excited children all but burst out. Just as eagerly, the moms looked forward to the weekly afternoon of fun. After all, they'd been friends since junior high, and they almost felt like sisters.

For the first time, however, the moms' friendships were about to be threatened. This week's session was at the home of Kate, mother of young Matt—a child to whom Laila, Monica, and Lisa, with much guilt but in complete agreement, privately referred as "the Brat." Matt was an ill-behaved child with whom even a sister would find it challenging to spend time.

The group approached the front door, chatting merrily. Laila noticed Jennifer clutching her new stuffed bunny tightly; her daughter seemed apprehensive. Laila tried to cheer her up, promising a fun day. The notion faded as quickly as the sound from the doorbell; Matt opened the door barely the width of the chain lock, peeked at them, stuck out his tongue, and slammed the door shut. The group didn't have to strain to hear Matt's giggling, followed by Kate's admonishment: "Matt, *huuuhh-neee*, I told you before not to do that. It hurts people's feelings. Not only that," she continued, "but it embarrasses me. Why do you embarrass me, Mattie?"

If Matt responded to his mother, no one on the other side of the door heard it. The moms exchanged looks, their eyes saying it all.

Kate opened the door and made an effort to greet her guests as though nothing had happened. She encouraged the kids to run off to the playroom and invited her friends to the kitchen for a companionable cup of java.

Not five minutes later, Kimmy rushed into the kitchen, Matt right behind. Kimmy tried in vain to explain what happened through her tears, but Matt interrupted repeatedly with "I didn't do anything!" and "It wasn't my fault." The moms finally deduced that Matt wouldn't let Kimmy touch any of his toys and had defended his possessions rather physically.

Kate put her arm around her son and whispered, "Matty, sweetie, please go play nicely for a while. The grown-ups want to visit. You really need to learn to share your toys so that Kimmy will want to come over and play with you again. Now, go share your toys with her, OK, *huhhhh-neee?*" Kate gently directed Matt toward the playroom, hoping that the rest of the visit would go smoothly—but suspecting otherwise.

The children wandered off, Kimmy sulking and Matt grinning victoriously, since he had no intention of sharing anything with anybody, and knew that nobody was going to make him. The other moms sipped coffee, trying hard to enjoy a few minutes of each other's company and to ignore the first battle in what they knew would be an ongoing war. It wasn't long before the next salvo was fired. Matt was back, and he began rooting through a kitchen cabinet. Kate asked in a singsong voice, "Whatcha looking for, sweetie? No snacks now. Too close to suppertime."

"I'm not gettin' nothin'," he mumbled. The odd bulge under his shirt shouted something else. His exasperated mother got up and lifted his shirt, releasing a bag of chips and a carton of cookies. Matt mustered a poorly feigned look of shock. The other moms peered awkwardly over their coffee cups and listened, again, to the singsong voice Kate used to talk to her son.

"Matty, sweetheart. You know I don't like it when you lie to me. And you're not supposed to take food into the playroom." Her sentences ended on a high note, as if she were posing a question. He mumbled his obligatory "sorry" and rushed off, leaving the pilfered goods on the floor. Kate was stretched thin between embarrassment at her son's conduct and her frustration with her constant (and futile) begging for good behavior. She wondered why *her* child was the only one to wreak havoc on what should be a pleasant afternoon.

A few minutes of peace and friendly conversation passed as the moms enjoyed their visit. But all too soon, a wail stopped them cold; with motherly swiftness, they sped to the playroom, gaping at the scene. Jennifer's new and much-loved stuffed bunny now looked more like a hedgehog. The scissors in his hand and pile of fur by his feet betrayed Matt's guilt but aroused no discernible shame. Laila was speechless. She hugged her sobbing daughter as the other moms returned silently to the kitchen.

Kate reprimanded Matt in a harsh tone this time. "Matthew! Shame on you! You know better than to ruin someone else's toy! And you're not allowed to use my scissors! What am I going to do with you? Why can't you just behave?" Matt was facing her as she spoke, but the blank expression in his eyes proved that her words were not sinking in.

Kate turned to Laila and Jennifer and blubbered an apology on her son's behalf. The remainder of the visit was short and tense. One by one, the moms suddenly "realized the time" and left for more peaceful homes.

The Hidden Message

"I can't control you. I don't know how to set boundaries for your behavior. I don't know how to persuade you to behave. So, go ahead and do whatever you want—all I'll do is fret about it."

Think About It

The problem with Matt goes so much deeper than his not wanting to share, taking food without asking, damaging a friend's toy, or being disrespectful. The real problem is that Matt doesn't know what rules he should live by, what behavior is expected of him, what the consequences would be for nonobedience—or if any would ensue at all. His mother's gentle scoldings and exasperated words are not enough to give him the information he needs. A "brat" like Matt is not born in a day. Behavior like his develops slowly, each day building upon the one before; each negative behavior that is ignored or inappropriately handled contributes to an overall family climate, a torture zone in which the child continues to misbehave and the adult continues to pay lip service to it.

Matt and all other children are remarkably astute. They figure out from a young age just how much power their parents have over them—or don't. If parents impose specific rules and enforce them with consistent and fair discipline, then children learn how to behave appropriately. If parents fail to establish rules or to follow through, and their only response to misbehavior is to complain about it, they end up with a child who has difficulty behaving appropriately and whom people want to avoid. What his mother doesn't see—the real tragedy here—is that Matt is the person who will suffer most in the end.

Changes You Can Make

Children are not born knowing right from wrong, nor are they born with good manners and refined social skills. These are all proficiencies that they must learn. Parenting is a tough job, requiring a constant flow of teaching, directing, and correcting to equip our children to manage their own behavior someday. How well, and how quickly, they take over this job depends on how much training we give them and what kind. I suggest the following guidelines to achieve success in this area:

1. Accept the role of leader in your relationship with your child. In our story, Kate does not act as if she's in charge. Her admonishments to Matt are expressed in a weak,

pleading whimper. Her presentation does not communicate authority or confidence. As an example, when Matt would not share his toys, Kate pleaded with him, "Matty, sweetie, please go play nicely for a while. The grown-ups want to visit. You really need to learn to share your toys so that Kimmy will want to come over and play with you again. Now, go share your toys with her, OK, *huhhhh-neee?*" Instead, if Kate were to speak to him eye-to-eye in a firm voice, giving him specific instructions, Matt might just show more respect for her words. Kate would have conveyed more authority by placing her hands on Matt's shoulders, looking him in the eye, and stating her expectations: "Kimmy is our guest today. She came to play with you, and I expect you to share nicely with her."

2. Set clear rules. Being an effective leader for your child goes beyond imparting instructions. A good parent-leader will take the time to teach, to lay ground rules, and to explain expectations up front. Matt not sharing his toys is a very typical situation that can be avoided when a parent teaches and creates rules in advance. Kate could have devoted some time before the day of the play group session to detail the performance standards. She could then have tailored rules for Matt to follow. For example, "You may put aside a few special toys that you don't have to share, but everything else in the playroom is there for your friends to play with." Kate may even want to outline the consequences for not sharing—in advance. "If I find that you are not sharing, then you'll be sent to your room for a time-out while your friends play with the toys."

The more that your children understand in advance what you expect of them, the easier it is for them to comply. As noted, if Kate had described her expectations to Matt prior to the play group's arrival, he would have had rules to guide him. Even better, if their family had definite rules about sharing in general, Matt would learn a *pattern* of acceptable behavior. Another advantage to having specific rules is that, as a parent, you do not need to reestablish boundaries for every situation; the rules become a template for everyday interactions.

3. Follow through after your pronouncements. Children will test our authority over them—often and repeatedly. Our job is to ensure that our children follow our instructions. If Kate had given Matt her instructions beforehand, then reminded him of the policy when he didn't share, she could have then led him back to the playroom and supervised for a few minutes to make certain that he was sharing. If he did not cooperate, then he should be sent to his room for the promised time-out.

Learn new skills. Being a parent may well be the most challenging job you've ever had, and as with any other job, it can be done much more effectively with knowledge and skills. Learning more about what are "typical" behaviors, and how to handle those behaviors, can benefit you at every stage of your child's development. Learning how to use the many creative and worthwhile parenting skills that can be gleaned from parenting books, magazines, and classes can make your life much easier and can help make your job as parent much more pleasant and rewarding.

Balance of Power

When Michael arrived home from work, he found his wife, Sharon, pacing the floor. Her eyes were rimmed in red. Wadded tissues surrounded the ice cream carton on the kitchen table. "What's the matter, honey?" he asked.

"Everything!" she wailed. "I think I'm going to have to quit my job!" Michael was shocked and confused. Sharon had been at her job for only a month. She'd waited until their son, Jason, began kindergarten to go back to work; when she made the move, it was with a sense of glee mixed with firm commitment to making the whole process work well for her son. She even arranged a car pool with her neighbor. Maria would drop Jason off at his grandmother's house, where he'd spend a few hours after school before Sharon picked him up on her way home. It seemed an ideal arrangement: the job of her dreams (for which she'd spent months preparing and interviewing) and child care that was both convenient and trusted. Now Michael wondered what could have gone wrong.

Michael sent Jason out to the yard to play and sat down at the table with Sharon. "Ok. Tell me. What happened?" Sharon took a deep breath and began, "When I picked Jason up, Mom said things aren't going well. To start with, Maria complained to her that Jason's been fighting in the backseat with Tomo."

Sharon's face suddenly changed from sad to angry. "And I know where Jason's getting this behavior . . . I can't understand why Maria even agrees to take Tomo! He's such a bad influence on all the kids! He's always causing trouble. What does she expect if she's going to have him in the car? And besides, Jason is hungry right after school; he gets fussy. I asked Maria to let him have a snack on the way home, but she doesn't want the kids to eat in her new car."

"Well," Michael said slowly, "maybe I could rearrange my hours and take a later lunch. That way, I could pick Jason up and take him over to your mom's. What do you think?"

"Oh, honey, that would be wonderful," she managed, "but there's an even bigger problem." Sharon took another deep breath, looking more pained rather than relieved. Mom says that Jason is proving to be, oh, how did she word it? 'A handful'—that's what she said! She said, 'He disrupts my entire afternoon!' Well, what did she expect when she agreed to take care of him? I've tried to explain that he's a spirited child, and that she'd have a much easier time if she took him over to the playground after lunch to work off all that energy, but she says it doesn't fit with her afternoon routine! I can't understand how difficult it would be for her to walk him two blocks to the park for half an hour! It's her own fault he won't settle down for her!"

Sharon sighed, as if to expel the unpleasantness of the situation. "*I* never have these problems with Jason. I think I'll just have to quit my job so I can be home with him."

The Hidden Message

"You aren't responsible for your own behavior; you're not capable of self-control. No matter what the situation, the blame for your misbehavior falls with someone or something beyond your control. It's not *you*—it's *them*."

Think About It

When parents routinely blame outside influences for their child's misbehavior, its source is placed beyond the child's control. "He can't help it!" becomes the daily mantra. The result is counterproductive: Excuses are made, and the child is not held accountable. The child feels helpless to control his own behavior and readily accepts the excuses made for him. Positive changes and growth never occur. In our story, Sharon is so busy placing blame for her son's behavior—on her mother, the car pool driver, the kid he sits next to—that she never acknowledges that some, most, or maybe even all of the responsibility for Jason's behavior should be handed directly to Jason. She never once thinks that these problems may be solved by changing not the world but Jason's own actions.

Children whose parents make excuses for them can carry this victim attitude into adulthood. "My neighbor's dog barks at night and keeps me up; that's why I'm late to work every morning." "My knee injury prevents me from exercising; that's why I'm out of shape." "My father was an alcoholic; that's why I can't keep a job."

The most common reason that parents fall into this trap? Parents often find child rearing to be a much bigger job than they ever expected. Couple that with the typically blind and consuming love of the average parent, and you can see why blaming outside influences is easier than believing the child capable of disappointing his parents with his misbehavior. Plus, changing the child's unwanted behavior can be difficult and time consuming, so it's natural to want to shirk this overwhelming task.

On the flip side, if we demand that our children take responsibility for their own behavior—regardless of peer influences, physical aptitude, or environmental pressures—they develop self-control, self-discipline, and a strong inner conscience to guide them in their lives.

Changes You Can Make

The most important concept to understand is this: You *can* expect your child to behave appropriately *regardless* of the outside influences in his life. Life will always pose challenges; we can show our children that they have the skills and ability to meet those challenges. The key is to strike the correct balance of power. In other words, you must give your child the power to control his own behavior, while you develop a parenting style that sets the boundaries for your child until he can set them for himself.

You can, and should, acknowledge the power of peers, teachers, television, learning and behavior disabilities, and the myriad other influences in your child's life. You can take into account the impact of these elements on your child's life. This does not mean, however, that you should confer on them the power to become excuses for poor conduct.

Compensate for these influences by modifying your parenting approach based on your keen knowledge of your child's surroundings and personality. For example, if your child is high-energy, is spirited, or has been diagnosed with attention deficit hyperactivity disorder (ADHD), learning more about the condition will help you manage its ramifications. You may, for instance, begin to see the merit of writing down house rules for your child, developing daily routines, and articulating exact consequences for certain misbehaviors. In doing so, you help your child develop the self-control necessary to thrive in this world.

In our story, Sharon understands her son, but instead of using this knowledge to work with him, she uses it to excuse him. Sharon would be wise to concede that the world will not modify itself to meet Jason's needs—he must modify his behavior to find success in the world. Her goal should be to help Jason "fit in" to his surroundings. What are some of the ways she might do this? One is to spend time with Jason creating rules that apply during his car pool ride and his time with his grandmother. The better he comprehends what behavior is expected of him, the easier it will be for him to conform. Once the rules are set and fleshed out, Sharon should remind Jason of them daily—not as a lecture but as casual morning conversation. "Jason, remember that when you are at Grandma's, you should . . ." Then she should write down the rules and provide Grandma with a copy of them, along with a request that she help Jason remember to abide by them.

For some children, and Jason may be one of them, this process of outlining your specific expectations through rules is enough to make a positive difference in the child's behavior. For other children, though, you may need to take one more step. This is to specify—and follow through on—consequences for failure to adhere to the rules, and positive incentives for obeying them. For example, if Jason does not follow the rules, he may lose his television privileges over the weekend. If the rules are followed all week, Jason may earn the privilege of going out to lunch with Daddy on Friday.

As you can see, this technique puts Jason in the driver's seat. It gives him a format to follow until he is mature enough to develop self-control.

Making our children ultimately responsible for their own behavior doesn't hinder them. Instead, it frees them to achieve success, unencumbered by the frailties that can readily derail a less-disciplined person, and it helps them to find confidence and happiness in their lives when they reach adulthood. Isn't this one of our highest goals as parents?

Preschool Instructions

It was a typical recess at Family House Preschool: children scattered around the open courtyard, high-pitched squealing and giggling. Keeping watch over the playground, Miss Sally—one of the teachers—noticed two children breaking one of the playground rules. She strolled over to remind them, "Hey, you guys, remember the rule! Don't climb on the fence!" The kids jumped down. Thinking she could capitalize on the exchange to prevent another transgression, she added, "And don't forget our other climbing rule: Don't climb the sign pole!" She walked away, watched by a quick and wiry four-year-old from the vantage point he had just assumed about four feet up—on the sign pole.

Miss Sally turned toward the building to catch view of two little girls fighting over a tricycle. She approached just as one pushed the other. Ever patient, Miss Sally crouched down to remind them, "Girls! Please don't fight over the tricycle! If you don't stop, soon you'll be hitting each other, and then you'll be very sad." Just as Miss Sally withdrew to spot-check the swing set, she heard an unmistakable series of sounds: Whack! Waahhh! "Miss Sally!" Hand to her head, she retraced her steps to intercede in the tricycle war.

Lunchtime came quickly, as it always does. "Children!" Miss Sally called. "Time to head in for lunch! Let's go straight inside— no stopping to pet the bunnies on the way in." Sure enough, she had to redirect several of the little ones who just *had* to stop to pet the cute fur balls as they passed.

Miss Sally had finally gathered her charges to the table when she spotted one little boy beginning his lunch with a chocolate chip cookie. She laughed as she asked him to put the cookie down. "You're being silly! Don't eat dessert until after you eat your sandwich!" Behind her, next to her, across from her, she witnessed a legion of preschoolers feasting on a first course of cookies.

After lunch, the class was humming with activity. Children pursued various creative endeavors, teachers hovering over little shoulders. Tiny Heather was attempting to draw a picture when she realized that her pencils were stubs in need of a good sharpening. She ambled over to the pencil sharpener. Methodically working her way through the pencils, she was delighted when Miss Sally walked by and asked her to take care of the job of emptying the sharpener's barrel. The teacher had one more thought: "Oh, and please remember not to empty it into the wicker trash basket."

"Ok," Heather nodded. After five minutes of intense sharpening, she walked past the metal trash can and emptied the shavings into the wicker basket.

The Hidden Message

"I'll give you *lots* of ideas of interesting things to do, things you might not have thought up without my help. They're all preceded by the word *don't*—which you can ignore."

Think About It

Don't think of a cow. Don't think of a tree. Don't think of ice cubes floating in a glass of water. Don't pay any attention to the saliva in your mouth or how often you swallow. Don't think of your breathing right now—breathing, in and out; don't think of it—breathing in and out . . .

I'm willing to bet that the last ten seconds have put a cow, a tree, and a few ice cubes in your head. And now you're thinking about swallowing, or the rhythm of your breathing, aren't you? (Unless someone has tried this trick on you before, I bet it's taking all your willpower not to think about that cow, a tree, some ice cubes, swallowing, and breathing.)

We humans are a funny lot, so subject to suggestion that we often are compelled to do exactly what we've been told not to do; the admonishment of "don't" sometimes has little sticking power. The mere mention of a forbidden fruit puts it front and center in our brains. (Ever been on a diet that forbids a certain type of food, only to fail miserably in a blitz of consumption of that food?) Multiply this effect tenfold if the human being in question is under the age of eighteen. The slightest mention of an intriguing new idea gets a child thinking of just how to effect it.

Changes You Can Make

Make a very simple, but powerful, change in the way you communicate to children. Instead of telling them what *not* to do, tell them what *to* do. Consider the difference between these statements:

Don't push your sister.	Be gentle with your sister.
Don't yell.	Use a quiet voice.
Don't run near the pool.	Walk!
Don't use that tone of voice with me!	I expect you to speak politely.
Don't dawdle on your way home.	Come straight home after school.
Don't forget your lunch.	Remember your lunch.
Don't touch the TV controls.	Here, you can play with this toy.
Don't stand on your chair.	Sit on your chair.

I could make the following suggestion: Don't use negative instructions. But that doesn't tell you what you *should* use in their place. Instead, if I were to use concrete and explanatory language, I'd increase the chances that you will follow my advice. So, this is what I'll say: Use positive language to communicate your expectations. Tell your children specifically what you want them to do. Use proactive expression, as opposed to prohibitive expression, because it transfers control—and opportunity—to the listener.

You'll see: when you replace negative reprimands with positive mandates, you give children the information they need to behave appropriately and the opportunity to do so. The decision to *use* that information is still theirs, but they're not left to guess at what your expectations are. You'll also generate a more pleasant mood in your home. And I guarantee that you'll enjoy hearing your own voice so much more!

Monsters Under the Bed

Monica was frustrated. For months, her son's bedtime adrenaline rushes had wreaked havoc on the family. The monsters living in Adam's closet and under his bed, ready to pounce as soon as he closed his eyes, reduced the normally exuberant, confident child to a puddle of tears at the mention of bedtime. Every single night, Monica and Adam endured an hour or more of monster-repelling strategies and rituals that ended in either fitful, exhausted sleep—or an extra person in Monica's bed.

Adam first became aware of the monsters on an ordinary night, as he and his mother were going through their regular bedtime routines. Suddenly, he expressed concern that some "thing" was hiding in his closet. Monica made a great show of opening the closet doors and, with a wave of her arm, pronounced that the only "things" in there were his clothes. But not even his all-powerful, wish-granting mommy could dispel the demons; he was sure that something else lurked—"There, see it? Behind my pants?"—among the neatly arranged outfits. No amount of hanger rearrangement or motherly reassurance could quell her little boy's paranoia. That night, with a heart that ached for her child and a head that ached too, Monica ended up sitting beside Adam until he fell asleep.

And every night since, Adam persisted in his claim that the "things" were still in his closet; they soon began taking up residence under his bed, or behind his dresser. Dismayed, Monica vigorously tried every suggestion that friends and family offered.

Grandma suggested posting a sign on the door, "No Monsters Allowed!" Adam liked the idea and toiled for several hours creating and posting a very authoritative sign—but apparently the "things" couldn't read. Aunt Lisa suggested "monster repellant" spray, so Monica filled a squirt bottle with water and allowed Adam to take it to bed. Adam's "things," however, had been vaccinated against such concoctions. Monica's friend suggested a flashlight and a night-light—which only created more shadows in which the "things" watched and waited. A neighbor suggested reading the classic *Where the Wild Things Are*, in which a boy befriends the monsters in his room. But Adam was quick to explain the nature of his "things," who were not the friendly type. Worse, the book's elaborate pictures put a face on his "things"—he announced that they looked most like the creature who menaced page 17.

Monica's older and wiser brother Greg stepped up with an offer to "exorcise" the monsters. In cape and hat, he pranced about the room, fancifully muttering what, to Monica, most resembled pig latin. No luck, though. Adam discovered that his "things" would only leave while Uncle Greg was in the room and then return as soon as his uncle split.

Monica finally gave up. She put a sleeping bag on the floor next to her bed and a wish under her pillow that Adam would grow out of his fears, and hopefully, soon.

The Hidden Message

"Yes, Adam, there *are* monsters. And obviously, we are more scared of them than *you* are. So scared, in fact, that we're trying all these extravagant methods, and not even these work. Not even your mother can make them go away! You better stay here with me tonight; you have good reason to be afraid."

Think About It

Children harbor all kinds of peculiar fears rooted in the physical world: dogs, vacuum cleaners, thunder, strangers, foods touching each other on the dinner plate. Then there are the limitless demons produced by active imaginations and dessert too close to bedtime: ghosts, aliens, beasts, monsters—a virtual parade of terror-invoking encumbrances. We parents must teach our children how to discern between valid and imagined fears—and how to overcome them.

Many times, in our efforts to help our children overcome their fears, we inadvertently make things worse. By giving too much credence to fears of imaginary things, we actually validate them.

We make this same mistake in areas that extend way beyond a child's room. For example, consider the approach of hundreds of parents who leave sobbing children at preschools and day care centers; these well-meaning folks hug their children tightly, look into their pleading eyes, and pitifully voice consolations like "Oh, honey, don't cry. Everything will be OK; really it will." Then, most of these parents throw looks of concern and worry backward over hunched shoulders as they slink away—and every one of their children sees the looks and thinks, "Whoa! If *they're* so worried, I should *really* be concerned!" There are a lot of worried kids waiting for quitting time every day—but it doesn't have to be that way.

Changes You Can Make

Children always seem too busy to notice us adults while they're zipping here, playing there—but make no mistake: they are always watching, listening, taking it all in, looking for clues as to how the outside world should be interpreted. They rely on our signals to tell them if their fears are logical or if we are confident that things really will be just fine.

The premise of this discussion is children's imaginary fears; fears of actual entities or events—such as the fear of the impending death of a fatally ill family member, or the fear of riding in a car after a traumatic automobile accident—must be handled differently.

The most direct way to extinguish your child's fear of imagined threats is to not only *say* that things are OK, but also *act* as though they are. Don't overreact or yield the illusion any power, but at the same time, be sensitive to your child's feelings.

Balance your display of confidence with sensitivity, bearing in mind that, while the *object* of your child's fear is not real, the fear itself *is*. The situation calls for a more diplomatic and sympathetic approach than shoving your child to face his fear head-on, with a flip "There's no reason to be afraid." To laugh at or belittle him will only succeed in making him feel foolish; moreover, he will conclude that you are not his advocate—which is a scary thing indeed.

While many of Monica's tactics can be helpful in stemming "monster fears," all of them lumped together, combined with her intensity to solve the problem, actually made those monsters bigger than life. Depending on the circumstances, you can also employ other ghost-busting measures that Monica missed altogether.

There are ways to acknowledge your child's feelings of fear as being real while providing evidence that the object of the fear is imagined. Let him know that other kids have the same fears, and that people of all ages are sometimes afraid of things that they don't have to be afraid of. After that, see if you can figure out what's causing him to be fearful. These types of fears, which are very normal, are usually triggered by a growing child's exposure to the world and his confronting a host of new experiences. Likewise, a significant change in his life—a move to a new home, starting at a new school, bringing home a new sibling—can cause a disturbance in his thought patterns, resulting in new anxieties. It may help to talk with your child (not at bedtime!) about his life experiences and help him accommodate the many changes that occur as he grows up.

A new bedtime ritual can be beneficial too. A light snack, a soothing story, gentle music, happy talk, and a loving back rub may ease his mind enough for him to be able to fall asleep.

Help your child sort out the difference between real and imaginary. This is a discovery process that takes place over many conversations and is also a developmental process that is linked to your child's level of maturity. You might help this process along by discussing the differences between, say, a rabbit you see at the zoo, Bugs Bunny, a stuffed bunny, and rabbit he can imagine in his mind. You can talk about the images that form in his head as you read a book to him. You can contrast the difference between real creatures—like a dolphin—and imaginary creatures—like a mermaid. You can make an entertaining game of it for him: "Can a stuffed bunny eat your soup?" "Can a real bunny talk?" "Can you walk on the ceiling?" Show him that imagining something can't make it so.

Patiently help your child confront and overcome his anxiety. If dark shadows are creating the monsters, spend some time together in your child's room in the dark, picking out spooky shapes or suspicious shadows; make a game of guessing what they really are, then turn on the light to see who wins. It may be comforting to let your child drift off to sleep afterward with a light on, and turn it off before you retire.

To make the dark less mysterious, plan a few fun nighttime activities. A campfire or marshmallow roast, a stargazing walk, or a candlelight dinner will help your child make friends with the darkness.

If you follow all these suggestions, but your child is still fearful, it would be a good decision to enlist the services of a mental health professional who can help puzzle out the real reason for the fear and recommend the best solution for your child.

Yes, there *are* objects and events meriting fear in this world, and we must remember that the degree of our fear is directly proportional to our size. With careful thought and planning, and using the best solutions, you can help your child achieve victory over fears of the imagined—so that he can better do battle with the real fears that are an inevitable part of adulthood.

6

Messages About Listening and Caring and Love

Empty Your Hands,
Open Your Heart

"First thing when I got up, there she was," Becca began, "Savannah, my five-year-old journalist-to-be in her full question mode. The interrogation started: '*Why* are you putting on makeup? *What* is that pink stuff? *How* do you learn to put contacts in your eyes?' I suppose I should try to explain things, but most of my answers sounded like variations of the word *because*. My mind was on other matters; I had a busy day ahead of me.

"As she followed me to the kitchen, her prattle continued. 'Why do we have pancakes for breakfast? Angie's daddy makes them too, but she doesn't live with him all the time. I wonder if she has pancakes at her mommy's house too?' Since I was concentrating on making breakfast and making plans for the day, I admit it: I met her often long-winded, meandering comments with that two-syllable acknowledgement—'mmm hmmm'—that says 'I know you're there, but I'm too busy even to feign interest right now.'

"My little chatterbox was relatively quiet while she ate her pancakes, so I had a few minutes to return a phone call and make a shopping list. Soon, though, her mouth was empty of food and open for business. She was chattering about everything and anything—and I marveled that just a few short years ago, her vocabulary was limited to a handful of words! As I went about my morning routine, it seemed that she was popping up around every corner. I was immersed in my daily chores and granted her a few 'mmm hmmms' along the way.

"I traipsed down to the kitchen to clean up, and there she was too, standing beside me as I washed the dishes and tidied the kitchen. My mind was wandering, when I realized she was being pretty persistent about telling me something. I felt her little hands tugging on my shirt as she intoned, over and over, 'Mommy, I want to tell you something. Mommy, listen. Mommy. Mommy.' Finally, in a frustrated huff, which I know was not warranted, I threw down the sponge and knelt down in front of her. In a tone a bit more clipped and a voice quite louder than intended, I looked her in the eye and demanded, '*What*?!'

"Not noticing—or perhaps not *caring* to notice—my short temper, my unflappable little one was breathless with excitement. She exclaimed, 'Mommy, Mommy, I need to tell you something!'

"I couldn't decide if her delight stemmed from the urgency of her message or from my sudden interest, but it didn't matter anyway. She stumbled over her words in her haste. 'Mommy, *this* is *so* exciting . . .' And as she screwed up her mouth to blurt out her news, she unexpectedly stopped in midsentence, taking on a look of puzzlement and intrigue. She stared at me as though she'd discovered the New World. 'Wow, Mommy, your eyes are really, really pretty blue!'

"My shame hit me like a brick: how little eye-to-eye listening could I have been doing for her not to have noticed the color of my eyes? I tell you, my blue eyes filled with tears as I hugged my little girl. I really do need to spend more time just listening."

The Hidden Message

"What you have to say is not important enough to justify my complete attention."

Think About It

It's an overwhelming task, this growing up. As children make their ways through the maturation process, they encounter new concepts every single day. And no matter how delightful the discovery, they must integrate each one into their understanding of the world at large and how it relates to them. All this life work often results in self-doubt and confusion. Adding to that is the judgment and criticism that sometimes seem to emanate from all corners of their lives—their teachers, their friends, their peers, the media. Perhaps the harshest assessments eventually come from themselves. When life feels overwhelming, children first seek the safe, secure refuge of their parents' arms . . . and the understanding audience of their parents' ears. Yet, all too often they meet only more judgment and criticism, or worse yet, impatience and indifference. And when this happens, they wander on in bewilderment, hoping to find someone who will withhold judgment and offer the attention they crave.

Our local newspaper interviewed 100 kids, aged seven to seventeen. They were asked, "What do you wish your parents did differently?" The most common answer? No, it was not more junk food, later curfews, or unlimited TV privileges. The most common answer, at all ages, was "I wish they would listen to me." When kids want parents to listen to them, they don't mean listen and judge, listen and nag, or even listen and solve. What they mean is, they would like their parents' attention and interest. Too many times, parents tell children that they'll talk "later" or "in a minute"—but later never comes. Typically, when your child wants your attention and you respond quickly and totally, your child's needs will be met. If, however, your child must wait endlessly for your attention, the problem will grow as she waits, or even worse, she'll take her thoughts to someone else, and you'll never even know what you've missed.

Equally important as the basic service of listening, parents are wise to listen with the attention and thought that allows them to understand what they hear. Children aren't always accurate and articulate when they talk. Parents need to listen for the real meaning—listen between the lines. Even as young adults, our children sometimes deliver words that are very different from their intended meaning. It's an astute parent who can get past the literal words being spoken to reach the heart of the matter. We sometimes find this hard to do because we get caught up in our child's tone of voice or manner of speaking. Or we make up our minds quickly, as we assume that the conversation will be a copy of past experiences. Or we're too distracted by our own thoughts to pay much attention to theirs. My oldest daughter, Angela, was once trying to explain something to her dad, who was busy completing a project on his computer. At one point, she accused him of not listening. He said that he *was* listening. Her answer? "Daddy, you're listening, but you're not understanding."

A smart parent will try to get beyond the act of listening and move toward real comprehension. Of course, there will be moments, like this one between Angela and her dad, when we aren't up to par in the area of listening. We just need to make certain that these times are the exception, rather than the rule. Obviously, and luckily, Angela is used to getting her dad's attention and is comfortable enough to be able to voice her displeasure when she doesn't!

Steven Vannoy, in his masterful book *The 10 Greatest Gifts I Give My Children,* writes: "If you think it's difficult to find the time to listen *now,* I assure you that the pain of being cut off from the essence of those beautiful children when they stop talking to you will make you wish you'd found the time and the willingness to listen earlier." A heart-wrenching example presented itself recently when I was the featured guest for an on-line group chat. I noticed one person who had logged on but was quietly monitoring without participation. Finally, she joined in: "I'm thirteen, and I just found out I'm pregnant. My parents don't ever listen to me or understand me, and I'm afraid to tell them. I don't know what to do." This desolate child was so desperate for an understanding adult to talk to that she presented her very personal problem to a stranger during an on-line chat!

Granted, that example is a far cry from the excited revelations of a five-year-old—but vital connections between parents and adolescents first take shape in early childhood. Every parent should hope and pray to keep a door open through which their children can enter with every problem or thought—whether it be a new tale to tell or an unplanned pregnancy. But the hopes and prayers that frame up that door will mean little unless they're hammered together with the powerful action of listening.

Changes You Can Make

In giving us each two ears and one mouth, our Creator certainly has made his position clear: none of us would suffer if we'd spend twice as much time listening as we do talking. Of course, we are remarkable creatures capable of multitasking. We can engage in many manual functions under a barrage of audio input and output, but listening, like our ears, should always be closer to the top of things. Nowhere is this truer than in the arena of child rearing, where attending to the details of our daily lives can often preclude really listening to our kids.

We give our children an indelible message of love and acceptance when we truly listen to them. Listening is not a passive activity; if you want to hone your skills in true listening, first put down the paper or the dish towel, shut off the TV, turn away from the computer screen. Get eye-to-eye and heart-to-ear. Tune in to not only the words but also the meaning and person behind them. Give your child the time necessary to complete a thought without your feeling that you must jump in to solve, predict, answer, or lecture. And remember that, often, your children don't want, or need, advice. They need you to empty your hands, open your heart, and truly listen to what they have to say.

When you have achieved this level of listening, many benefits tumble forth. Your children will talk to you about both the highlights and lowlights in their lives without fear of judgment or criticism. They will become more honest and open. And perhaps, as a clincher, you will have an opportunity to share your thoughts and values with a child who knows how to listen, because she has learned from experience.

How do you know that you're a successful listener? At the end of each week, take this little performance quiz. See how many statements you can honestly mark with a "Yes." Although you'll rarely be able to affirm all seven in a week, the more you can answer yes, the better:

1. I looked into my child's eyes as I listened.

2. My child told me something I didn't know.

3. I asked my child a question and then listened to the entire answer without interrupting.

4. I put down whatever was in my hands to show my child my full attention.

5. I was available to my child when he or she wanted to talk to me.

6. As I listened to my child, I held back at least one unproductive comment.

7. I laughed at something funny that my child said.

The Shoebox

Deanna, with a mixture of pride and wistfulness, was helping her son, Kyle, pack for college. Together, they folded clothes into boxes and took posters off of walls as he talked eagerly of his upcoming adventures. His enthusiastic monologue halted, however, when Deanna pulled from under his bed a tattered shoebox, held together with five thick rubber bands. "I'll take that, Mom," he muttered, as he snatched the box from her hands.

Too stunned to speak, Deanna carefully regarded the boy who, up until now, shared much of his inner self with her freely. Her thoughts meandered through the past eighteen years, which replayed themselves like a sweet old movie, happy memories flickering by in shades of gold. There was Kyle as he took his first steps and landed in her arms. Oh, and there she was, teaching him, again, about—was it poisons this time? Or hot burners? Wait, he looked older there; that must have been the "bad strangers" talk. The setting switched to his room, with the both of them perched on his bed, talking, laughing, and sometimes crying about friendships and girls and school and pimples. It was a movie she could watch again and again. And always—always!—there were those little yellow notes . . .

They were sometimes just hellos, or reminders of her pride in her son's accomplishments. Sometimes, they were intended to cheer up a bleak day. Some merely assured her son that she was thinking of him. They were silly, lyrical, unexpected snippets of her heart, stuck onto the ordinary objects that populated his day: cereal boxes, a much despised history book, his worn baseball glove, and more recently, the steering wheel. Somehow, leaving those little adhesive notes became a regular part of their lives. No matter what the occasion, during good times and not-so-good, one common thread ran through their days together: a mother's undying and unshakable love, expressed in those little innocent notes.

She smiled and reluctantly turned her thoughts back to matters at hand. Her smile faded a bit as she spied that closely guarded shoebox. What could he be hiding from her? Why was he being so secretive? Had she said enough about cigarettes and sex and drugs? Had she taught him how to protect himself? Had she taught him enough about life? She thought that she'd done a good job—that she'd always left the door open for him to talk about anything on his mind.

But there was that box.

She continued helping him pack and tried to keep her spirits light, but her eye kept traveling over to the tattered cardboard mystery he'd now shoved in the corner between his dresser and the wall.

Later that week, Kyle was gone. He'd slipped out of her arms and into a world from which she could no longer protect him, seeking an education and a life. True, she also now was free to pursue a new life. Like her son, she had bent her mind relentlessly around the possibilities that awaited after he'd left home.

On the morning of the second day after he'd left, Deanna sat at the kitchen table sipping coffee, wondering what Kyle was up to. Had he hung up his shirts as soon as he'd arrived, so they wouldn't wrinkle? Did he remember the "care package" she'd filled with potato chips, sodas, and other late-night study-fest fare? Had he made friends, good friends with decent values?

Had he found the note she'd stuffed between his folded jeans? It quoted a line from a favorite book she had first read to him when he was barely four. She remembered how hard it had been to read through the tears that flowed down her cheeks, and his puzzled look that asked why a child's book would make his mommy cry. But that book became a special, honored part of their bedtime routine, so she had copied from it and slid the note into his suitcase, which was now sitting in his new college dorm:

I'll love you forever,
I'll like you for always,
As long as I'm living
My baby you'll be. *

Her thoughts wandered back to all those notes from his childhood and adolescence. Had they made any impact? She figured if they'd brought just one dimple to his cheek, the little time and effort they took was more than worth it.

She couldn't get her mind off her son, so she thought she'd go tidy up what was left of his belongings in his room. She trudged up the stairs, feeling old and not quite as needed this morning. His room was too quiet, too tidy, too different, too *empty* . . . except for a cardboard box, forgotten in the corner between the dresser and the wall.

That blasted shoebox. What could be in it that he'd concealed for so long? Did it harbor explicit sex magazines? She hoped not; she thought she'd helped him learn respect for women. Or was it a secret stash of cigarettes, or marijuana, or worse? She replayed in her mind the many conversations they had about drugs, and hoped he had learned from them. Did the box contain something even more dangerous? What would he hide from her so pointedly? She glared at the cover, wishing she could see through it— to what? Could it be love notes from a girl? She smiled at the thought. But, now, she had to know.

---

*These quotes are from *Love You Forever*, by Robert Munsch (Firefly Books, 1986). If you haven't read this special children's book, hunt one down. (Oh, and get a tissue.)

Wracked with guilt, Deanna snatched the box from its hiding place and slipped off the rubber bands. She removed the cover and peered inside. The contents took her breath away, and she began to cry the great weeping tears that mothers cry, heaving heartfelt sobs from the depths of the soul.

It was filled with love notes, all right. *Her* notes, tied together with a ribbon he'd saved from the edge of his old baby blanket. She lifted the bundle of paper, turned it over in her hands, and ruffled through the pages; some were faded with age, some were only weeks old.

Deanna sat on the edge of the bed reading the old notes and weeping. She reached over to the top of the dresser for a tissue and spied a . . . yellow sticky note. But it was not one she had written. It was scrawled in her teenaged son's messy print and was obviously penned just a few days earlier:

I'll love you forever,
I'll like you for always,
As long as I'm living
My "Mom" you'll be. *

He'd copied from the very same book from which she borrowed the message she'd tucked in his luggage earlier that week, a book that she'd read to him since he was four years old, so long ago.

The Hidden Message

"My love for you is undying and unwavering. In small ways, and in all ways, I'll pass this message on to you."

Think About It

We shower our babies with signs of unconditional love. We snuggle and kiss and say "I love you" as often as it occurs to us to do so. As they grow up, though, the day-to-day business of living intrudes upon that spontaneity. Sadly, sometimes we *assume* that they know how much we care—that it's obvious with every car pool that we drive, every baseball game at which we cheer, every sock that we wash. But children are constantly challenged with the business of growing up. In that challenge, they suffer the pains of self-doubt, pains that can be relieved by a parent's daily displays of love. Generous displays of affection are to a child's soul what nutritious food and restful sleep are to his body, building him up and buffering him against the tribulations of growing up. A lack of these loving displays leaves your child weakened in the soul, with a day full of "do this" and "don't do that" and "don't forget" and "do it now." Necessary messages, I know, but to a child, they don't exactly convey unconditional love!

How many beautiful thoughts have you had about your children this week? *How many have you shared?* Surprising, isn't it, how many times our children delight, amaze, and otherwise touch us. And how seldom we tell them! How many times we watch our children quietly playing or reading and feel our hearts filling with love, yet remain mute in our admiration! Or we watch our child actually put his socks in the hamper, and we think, Well, look at that! What a great kid! But we don't say it. Perhaps we gaze at our children and reminisce about the days when they were soft babies—but we do so in the solitude of our mind's eye. All of these loving thoughts deserve to be shared with your child. And your child needs them. They are the words that help build a protective wall against the onslaughts in a child's—and later, an adult's—life. They are the words that help form self-esteem and a sense of being truly, completely loved—and they are eminently portable.

Changes You Can Make

Next time you glance at your child and *think*, "Look at that sweet face—I sure do love her," open your mouth and *say*, "Honey, you have the sweetest face; I sure do love you." Next time you witness socks getting hurled into the hamper, go ahead and *say*, "Wow! What a great kid you are!" How about a note saying "Sweet dreams, my wonderful child" placed upon a freshly made bed? Why not stick a note of encouragement in the pages of a textbook waiting to be studied? Or a note of confidence stuck to the inside of a violin case on its way to a recital? Or one of humor in a lunch pail? Surely, it would be every bit as nourishing as a peanut butter sandwich. How long would it take? And what could it hurt? *Why not?*

Once you start, you'll find hundreds of opportunities in the course of a regular day to reinforce those feelings of unconditional love. And there's nothing stopping you from expressing them. So, go ahead! Grab a pen and grab of few of these opportunities— and you may someday find a tattered shoebox under *your* teenager's bed.

Baby Love

Linda turned off the clock radio and tiptoed down the stairs. She flicked on the coffeemaker and settled herself in at her computer. The early-morning stillness reminded her anew of how much she enjoyed this peaceful time, when she was the only one awake. Another reason she loved being up first: she could relish the sounds of her home coming to life, sounds unique to every household.

As if on cue, the baby monitor on the corner of her desk telegraphed an end to the silence. Linda could easily mistake the tentative little coos for those of the mourning doves outside, if not for the fuzzy static that accompanied the tiny baby's babbling. After one quick sip of her coffee, Linda headed upstairs, hoping to get to the baby before her failure to appear transformed the gentle coo into a piercing wail.

Reaching the nursery in plenty of time, Linda picked her soft pink bundle up out of the crib and carried her over to the changing table. The mother took pleasure in her morning routine of changing, powdering, and dressing her little one for the day. The house was still chilly; Linda was grateful for the baby-wipe warmer she'd received as a shower present. As soon as their routine was completed, Linda dropped a soggy packet into the diaper disposal unit, turned off the electronic musical screen that kept Joy amused during the change, and plodded back downstairs.

"Time to make breakfast," she said to her smiling baby, who understood little but the possibility of a snuggle. Linda settled Joy into her favorite bouncy seat, which was placed close to the counter so Joy could watch Mommy prepare meals. Linda chattered to Joy as she bustled from microwave to toaster to stove. Just as she finished, another morning sound greeted them in the kitchen: the pitter-patter of big brother feet. Those feet brought Ethan first to Mommy for a hug and kiss, then up on tiptoes to kiss the significantly smaller toes of his baby sister. "Put Joy in swing?" he asked, as he always did in the morning.

"Sure, sweetie," Linda answered. "Good idea. That'll give me a minute to get a couple things done." She moved Joy over to the baby swing and watched in delight as Ethan made up songs to the rhythmic cranking of the musical swing.

Linda deposited a few utensils in the dishwasher and set the table for breakfast. Once Ethan was settled in his booster seat and Joy in her high chair, the three of them enjoyed a few golden moments of family life, the kind we think of as ordinary at the time but as magical in retrospect. Ethan always found Joy hysterical, squealing with delight at her innovative Cheerio-harvesting efforts; this morning, as usual, Joy came through, discovering her tongue to be a handy alternative to the chubby creased fingers that never seemed to close in on those elusive O's. (Of course, once her cheeks were sporting enough drool, the whole-face method worked best of all.)

After cleanup, Linda packed the kids up to accompany her on a few errands. On the way to the shopping center, a smiling Linda peeked in the rearview mirror often, watching Ethan entertain Joy. With their car seats side by side, it was easy for Ethan to lean over and make her toys dance and sing. Linda considered Ethan as sweet and funny as his baby sister did. He reveled in his big brother role, despite the occasional rubber cow whack to the face, such as he was cheerfully accepting today.

When they arrived at the shopping center, Linda popped out Joy's car seat and secured it in the strolling base, waiting patiently as Ethan—the world's newest do-it-yourselfer—unbuckled his seat belt and climbed down out of the van. Linda let Ethan walk and lead the way for a while, until his slow pace and intense interest in every passing object threatened to turn the morning's errands into a weeklong event. "Come on, buddy," she cajoled, "How 'bout a ride in the stroller?" She settled him into the toddler seat behind Joy, and they completed their day's tasks in no time.

On the way home, Joy and Ethan both fell asleep in their car seats. Linda smiled a mother's smile at the site of Joy's little sleeping face, with its bow-shape lips curled in a smirk that bespoke some pleasant reverie, cheeks rosy and soft as the peaches they'd just bought. She gingerly scooped her up, dreams and all, and carried her into the house.

After another trip to the car for her "big boy," Linda settled Ethan in his bed and Joy in her crib. In a trice, she was back at her desk, finishing up her work—but not for long.

Again, the baby monitor came alive with sound. Linda sailed back to Joy's room, and discerned that, sure enough, Joy's nap was a brief one. Linda, giggling at the grateful nose-burying ritual that her little daughter was performing, took Joy downstairs and put her in her playpen. Keeping an eye on Joy, she settled herself back down at her desk to finish her work. And thus, another day was passing in the rhythm of life.

The Hidden Message

"Why should I carry you or hold you when I have all these modern baby contraptions to put you in?"

Think About It

Some call it a sign of progress. Some call it liberating. Some call it convenient. What is it? The myriad fancy, colorful baby carriers that can contain your baby in every conceivable situation and position. Bouncers, jumpers, rollers, seats, strollers, and swings.

A virtual arsenal of inconvenience-fighting ground forces. But what do they provide from a baby's point of view? A soft, warm embrace? (No, a cold, hard surface.) The essential and nurturing touch of love? (No, an unyielding plastic structure.) A feeling of unassailable safety? (No, a strange feeling of being near those you love and need but too far away to receive comfort or get their attention.) Easy access to Mommy's touch, her breast, her loving face? (No, too much distance from Mommy to even see her face.)

Research proves over and over that we human beings crave touch and physical closeness. Babies make their love of contact obvious though their cuddles and wet kisses—how soon they learn to give these! Even those distant, sullen teenagers secretly love the physical attention they get from their parents (despite the kids' feigned protests). As adults, we continue to thrive on hugs, kisses, and other forms of affectionate human contact; we wither and die a little inside when our lives are void of these pleasures. Numerous books have been written about therapeutic touch and its power to heal emotional, as well as physical, hurts and ailments.

Jean Liedloff, in her fascinating anthropology book *The Continuum Concept* (Addison-Wesley Publishing, 1986), writes "The change from the total hospitality of the womb is enormous, but the infant has come prepared for the great leap from the womb to his place in arms. What he has not come prepared for is a greater leap of any sort, let alone a leap into nothingness, non-life, a basket with cloth in it, or a plastic box without motion, sound, odor, or the feel of life. The infant lives in the eternal now; the infant in arms in a state of bliss; the infant out of arms in a state of longing in the bleakness of an empty universe."

The most astounding proof that babies in particular have strong physical and emotional needs for loving touch is the success of a new way to care for premature babies: "kangaroo care." It's an approach that originated in Bogotá, Colombia, by neonatologists Edgar Rey and Hector Martinez. At the time of their study, the mortality rate of premature babies in Bogotá was 70 percent (this extremely high incidence is due to lack of power and reliable equipment). As part of the research on how to save more of these infants, the doctors had moms carry their preemies nearly twenty-four hours a day, seven days a week in specially designed sling carriers. The dramatic results? The mortality rate fell to 30 percent! Further studies by other scientists revealed that kangarooed babies had a more regular heartbeat, demonstrated a reduced need for supplemental oxygen, cried less, and spent more time in a deep sleep, thereby conserving energy for growth and development. A Neonatal Network study also reported increased intimacy and attachment between baby and parent under a kangaroo-care contact approach.

Katie Allison Granju, author of *Attachment Parenting* (Pocket Books, 1999), says that "human infants, like most mammal babies, are happiest, are most comfortable, and develop best when they are kept physically close to a warm body much of the time." Dr. William Sears, renowned pediatrician and my parenting hero (as described in the Foreword of this book), says, "It is a natural, appropriate, and desirable part of development for a baby to be dependent. A baby needs to bond with *people* before *things*." Frequent, appropriate touch builds bonds of trust that create security in an infant and independence in an older child. A baby who knows the world to be a safe, manageable place will more readily separate from his parents later, when appropriate, than a baby who has learned to fear separation early on. Consider, too, that the attachments you form with your baby set the stage for a connected lifelong relationship.

Given this resounding evidence, why would you want *your* baby to spend her day shuffled from one plastic container to another?

Changes You Can Make

It's eminently easy to change the pattern of behavior that has you installing your baby in a carrier. Pick up your baby. Smell her hair, kiss her butter-soft cheek. Hear her breath in your ear. Wrap your arms around her and sense the sum of her, this living, breathing expression of life. Realize that you have but a few short years to hold her this way, and that you will miss this when she's older— and so will she. Recognize that these moments are golden opportunities for you to know one another in a beautifully intimate way unique to childhood. Change your rationalizations about holding your baby, and soon you'll find yourself more and more often with that soft bundle in your arms. And it's habit-forming!

Of course, it's fine to use carriers and seats for your baby to make your life easier. And other than cases such as the premature newborns in the Colombian study, it's not practical or healthy to hold your child twenty-four hours a day. It all comes down to making wise choices about using these devices so that they don't become the prominent location for your baby's wakeful hours. You might even experiment with ways to blend convenience with touch. Try one of the many soft carriers that enable you to carry your baby while keeping both hands free to work around the house or office, shop, go for walks, tend to other children—so many activities can be easily done with you "wearing" your baby! Slings, frontpacks, and backpacks are available in many styles. A number of books discuss the pros and cons of each and offer instructions on how best to use them. If you'd like more information, check out *The Baby Book*, by Dr. William and Martha Sears (Little Brown, 1993), or *Attachment Parenting*, by Katie Allison Granju, as mentioned earlier.

Whatever tools you use to further the endeavor, do touch, hold, and cuddle your baby every chance you get. Give your toddler lots of hugs and kisses. Welcome your school-age child into your arms often. And laden that teenager with as much physical contact as he'll allow. And give some of that soul-enriching touch to your spouse, too.

The most wonderful thing about cuddling is that it is never unreturned. Don't believe me? Stop reading right now, and go

give your little one a good snuggle; I defy you to tell me you
didn't get cuddled back—and that you didn't love it.

The words of a poem called "Human Touch" by Spencer
Michael Free capture the spirit of this lesson:

> *It's the human touch in this world that counts,*
> *the touch of your hand in mine.*
> *For it means far more to the fainting heart*
> *than shelter, bread, or wine.*
>
> *For shelter is gone when the night is o'er*
> *and bread lasts only a day.*
> *But the touch of your hand and the sound of your voice*
> *lives on in my soul always.*

The Baseball Star

Baseball: it had been Frank's passion from his first swing of the bat in kindergarten up to the last home run in college. If he'd had his way, it also would be how he earned his living. But life took a different turn, and his sport was now a weekend hobby. He enjoyed participating in a local adult league, but his passion for the game centered now on sharing his knowledge and skill in his capacity as coach of his son Jeremy's team. The only sore spot for Frank was that Jeremy didn't have what it takes to be a star player—he didn't have what his father had. Frank couldn't zero in on the reason, but he found his son's athletic ability lacking when compared with his own in his youth.

On this day, Frank and Jeremy were getting ready to leave for practice. As was typical, Jeremy was dawdling. Frank's bellow could be heard throughout the neighborhood. "Come *on*, Jeremy! What's the holdup? Let's get moving! I hope you'll hustle better out in the field than you are here . . ."

On the way to practice, Frank delivered his typical pep talk. "OK, buddy, today I want you to use the form we practiced all weekend. If you keep that glove up, no ball will get by you. And remember, on those low ones, keep your glove on the ground, your eye on the ball, and your body in front of it. Got it?"

Jeremy was listening intently and nodding. "Yeah, Dad. I got it."

As usual, they were the first ones at the field. Jeremy helped his dad set up the equipment, then looked up to see several of his teammates arriving. With an OK from Frank, Jeremy ran off to exchange high fives and the day's hot news with his buddies. Frank watched the players, awkward in their suspension between boyhood and adolescence. One minute, they were giggling about some bodily function or pulling each others' caps down over their foreheads; the next found them chewing gum and looking tough, gathered for practice and ready to conquer. Frank preferred the latter.

After warm-ups, the boys set up in their fielding positions. As he always did, Frank stared at Jeremy and fervently replayed all his instructions in his mind like an endlessly looping soundtrack. Sometimes he almost believed that this little ritual would be enough to impel his son to move bat, ball, and body in the synchronicity that differentiates a star from a player. *"Use the form . . . keep that glove up . . . put your body in front of the ball . . ."*

"Dang! He missed the catch!" Frank could barely contain his frustration and annoyance as he watched his son race after the ball. With one graceful, powerful motion, Jeremy scooped it up just before it rolled under the fence, whirled around, and threw it to the cutoff player. *"Well,"* Frank thought, *"at least he knows where to throw it when he gets it."*

Batting practice followed. Jeremy's first swing missed the ball with that noise that basketball players love but that "the boys of summer" loathe: *swish.* Frank heard the other parents calling out to Jeremy, "Good swing!" and "Good form!" He wished he felt he had reason to yell such accolades; instead, he just watched, hoping his kid would actually hit the ball. Jeremy's next swing connected, but on a fly ball handily caught by their star player, Scott. "Way to go, Scott!" Frank cheered. *"Man,"* he thought, *"that kid never misses a catch. What a ballplayer."*

Between drills, Jeremy entertained the team with his familiar antics. The guys thought he was a riot. Some odd thing Jeremy had said doubled most of the players over in laughter once again, and Frank chuckled at the sight. He had to give the kid *that* much: Jeremy did have a great sense of humor. Frank just wished he was as gifted on the diamond . . .

After the water break, Frank called the boys out to the field. As he jogged toward the dugout for equipment, he heard two other dads talking. ". . . a real valuable player on the team," said one. "I'd say," agreed the other, "the kid's got guts." Frank couldn't help but feel an envious pang as he heard these men praising Scott. But he had to agree: the kid was a natural-born athlete. He never missed a ball, was always good for a double, and, in the last game, even managed a triple that was nearly a home run.

". . . A real heads-up player. He always knows what's happening on the field . . ." Frank agreed. And although he would never say it out loud, Scott reminded him of himself. Frank was a modest man, but his own strengths as a baseball player were undeniable. How he wished his Jeremy were a better athlete.

The conversation around him continued. ". . . As they say, the acorn never falls far from the tree!" Their elbow-jabbing laughter made Frank twitch.

"*Ahh*," Frank thought, "*so his dad's a player too. That explains a lot. Maybe I should look him up for the assistant coaching position that's opening next season.*"

Frank walked up behind the men, intending to ask about the baseball background of Scott's dad, when the next sentence he heard hit him like a hardball to the stomach. "I bet Frank's awfully proud. Jeremy's a real winner."

The Hidden Message

"I don't see you for who you are, I see you in light of who I want you to be."

Think About It

Even before our children are born, we begin to imagine what kind of people they will become. We envision "new and improved" editions of ourselves, who share our best strengths and lack our most despised weaknesses. But, unless you have somehow defied the usual methods of procreation, your little person will be, no doubt, very different from the Super-You conceived in your mind.

Changes You Can Make

Ask any parent about his or her kids, and you'll probably hear how they've each been born with personalities, interests, and traits incredibly different from those of their siblings—and of their parents. We can choose to bemoan these differences or to celebrate them. When we welcome the differences, when we see our children as individuals whom we can neither change nor re-create, we can enjoy them for who they are. Such acceptance within the family during childhood demonstrates that which must extend to the world at large in adulthood, and guards our children from forming relationships based on the hope of change.

We also have to resist the tendency to look to our children to fulfill some part of ourselves that we feel is missing, or to live out the dream that we never experienced. In Frank's case, he's hoping his son will pick up where he left off—and hoping Jeremy will end up having his picture hanging in the baseball Hall of Fame, most likely with a quote that he couldn't have done it without the help of his dad, the coach.

Shed your preconceived notions of the person you think your child should be or who you hope he will become, and accept and love your child for who he really is. Starting right now, look at your child with fresh eyes. Make the effort to find your child's best traits, enjoy the search, and treasure the discoveries. When you make a conscious effort to find the beauty in your child—the strengths, the unique and pleasant aspects of his personality—you will find a child blossoming anew in your eyes. And since children learn by example, your child might just be kinder in his assessment of *you* one day.

Begin now to remove the labels you've consciously, or unconsciously, given your child. "He's so lazy/selfish/thoughtless." "She is always forgetful/careless/bossy." "He's not much of an athlete."

"She never pays attention." Labels like these rarely encompass a whole child and often become self-fulfilling prophecies. If you continually single out the negative traits that you perceive in your children, they will begin to see themselves in the negative light you cast. And you will concentrate more and more on the episodes that prove these labels correct. Instead, put problems or negative traits in their proper perspective: "Jeremy struck out this time, but he was trying hard, and he's improved over last year." Or "Jeremy missed the catch, but he knows how to hustle after the ball, and he stays with it until he gets it to where it belongs." In some cases, your perspective may even have to be entirely different: "Kevin doesn't show any talent for baseball—but he has a good attitude and enjoys playing the game."

In our story, if Frank could understand that Jeremy does have strengths on the ball field but that they differ from his own, he would come to see his son as the other parents do. Frank had been looking for specific skills that he himself possesses and esteems. If he instead looks upon his son with an open mind and an open heart, he too will see that his son, in his very own way, is a valuable player on the team. And in the end, it doesn't matter as much how good a baseball player Jeremy is, but how good a person he is, and how good he feels about himself.

7

Messages About Time and Priorities

Daddy, Play with Me!

The clock in Jeff's car glows 6:40 P.M. as he rolls into the driveway after another long and tiring day at work. He opens the door to his home with a weary sigh and drops the mail next to the answering machine, which is blinking in that incessant, anxious way that demands listening. All he wants is a relaxing evening with no bosses, clients, or coworkers to please.

He peeks into his wife's home office and greets her warmly. As they chat about their day, she asks if he'd mind fixing dinner so she can finish up a few things. "No problem," he assures her. Before heading to the kitchen, he pauses to savor a moment's peace, silently planning out the next few hours: check the mail, listen to messages, take a nice hot shower, change into sweats, fix a quick dinner . . .

"Hi, Daddy! Play with me?" Snapped out of his reverie, Jeff puts on a smile and bends to wrap a hug around the giggling little angel with the hopeful eyes. He twirls her around in big circles and plants kisses on her nose. "Hey, my little Lily-flower!" he croons. He buries his nose in her soft hair, loving the little-child feel and scent of her. Laughing with glee, Lily cherishes these sparkling moments in her daddy's arms; craving more, she implores, "Play with me?"

"Hey, punkin', I have some things to do; then we'll play later."

"Just a *little* while, Daddy?" she pleads with a smile. But looking at his face, she suddenly knows he'd never drop everything just for some silly play, but she can't help asking one last time.

When the expected answer comes, she wanders off resignedly to watch the TV show that's always on at this time, always on for her when Daddy's not.

Lily watches her program, all the while counting the minutes on the clock. Jeff loses himself in the mail, the newspaper, and the answering machine, looking forward to the completion of all his daily responsibilities so that he can play with his daughter. After some time on the computer reading E-mail, he trudges upstairs, loosening his tie. He can almost feel the steamy warmth of the shower, the comfort of those old sweats, the . . . wait, what is *this*?

He turns to find a beaming little girl, who'd sneaked up the stairs behind him, given away by the soft thumping of her tiny feet. She musters all the vocal sweetness that she imagines a good girl to have and asks, "Can we play *now*, Daddy?" She doesn't want to bother him, doesn't want to pester. She just wants him close to her, laughing his silly laugh just for her.

What Jeff hears is persistence—a trait he will someday appreciate in her as an adult but one that annoys him today. So, with a ruffle of her hair, he dismisses her with strained patience. "In a little bit, Lily. Why don't you go ask Mommy if she can play with you now?"

Not so easily put off, she is in position at the bottom of the stairs when he descends some time later. Her little face is fairly bursting with the effort of holding back her request. She doesn't want to annoy him, doesn't want to be inconvenient, doesn't want to be bad—and so, says nothing, hoping he'll remember his promise to play "later."

But he doesn't.

"Ready for some dinner?" he asks, walking quickly past her in an effort to stave off a few repeats of her "Want to play?" chorus. He enters the kitchen and begins pulling items from the refrigerator. Just then, the telephone rings, and little ears listen—as they always do—as Jeff answers. "Hello? Hey, Steven. How are ya? Great. Did you catch the game Sunday? I can't believe he missed that play . . ." And so he is lost to her again, this time to adult conversation, phone tucked between ear and shoulder.

Maybe if I'm just quiet and smile real big, Lily thinks. So she looks up at him with every fiber of her being poured into her smile, every good thing in her soul spilling from her eyes. Still on the phone, her daddy smiles back vacantly and plops a plate of dinner down for his daughter, then disappears into his wife's office with a plate for her too. Lily's best smile fades as she quietly eats her dinner to the hum of Daddy's voice on the phone.

Afterward, of course, the parents are busy. There's dinner to be cleaned up, garbage to be taken out, bills to pay . . . And all the while, Jeff's little one—who naturally will not be little forever—patiently and proudly waits beside her latest Lego masterpiece. She just *knows* he'll notice it soon. She knows it's a marvel of engineering brilliance that is sure to draw him into her world. But the doorbell rings, and Jeff strides right past her to answer. Perhaps after the visitor leaves, she wonders . . .

It's Rahul, their neighbor. He needs help getting his lawn tractor started. "Hate to bother you, Jeff, but you think you might have a second to look at it?"

"Of course," Jeff replies, his thoughts registering the day last week when Rahul was there at 6:00 A.M. to jump-start his car. "That's what good neighbors are for."

After letting his wife know where he's bound, he reaches down to plant kisses on his daughter's soft cheeks. "Be right back, punkin'," he says. And he leaves too quickly to notice the silent tears that have begun to run down those same cheeks so hastily kissed, soft cheeks that are soon buried in pillows. When Jeff returns, she is asleep, dreaming of moving out and becoming a neighbor who can ring the doorbell, call Daddy on the phone, and send E-mails to him.

The Hidden Message

"You are not as important to me as the mail, the messages, the dinner, the phone call, or the neighbor. I love you, but I'm too busy for you—and there's always later, there's always tomorrow."

Think About It

Children perceive time, and what we do with it, differently from the way adults do. By about age thirty, we adults barely notice the precious seconds. In the currency of time, they're mere pennies, hardly able to buy anything of value. For little ones, however, every moment is weighty with possibility and thus passes heavily and slowly. Consider, for instance, the evening that we just witnessed—it passed particularly slowly for the little girl, but it blew past the man who is her father.

Seconds become minutes, of course, and minutes become hours, and imperceptibly, hours become decades. One day, Jeff may turn around to play with his little girl, only to find a young woman too busy tending to her own life to notice—after all, she has learned by his example. What a common tragedy! Ask any parent of grown children, and he or she invariably will attest to how fast it all goes. As the popular maxim forewarns: One comment you'll never hear on a person's deathbed is "I wish I'd have put in more overtime." Instead, we all know the final plea is much more likely to be for more time with those whose love fills us. The hard truth is that we have only a relatively small sliver of time in which to give our children the gifts of our experience, patience, wisdom, and heart.

Naturally, obligations intrude on our every day. We perceive these obligations from an adult point of view, sorting through them, prioritizing as we go. We give a potential interruption to our mental calendars a quick once-over and make a snap decision: adjust the plan, or stick to it? But however we triage the callings in our lives, time marches on. The work gets done. The meals get prepared. The house gets cleaned. Things work out. Of necessity, we allot time for the chores that keep us fed, clothed, clean; these occupations push themselves into our plans by their very nature. Other items seize our attention with their urgency— a flashing message machine, a ringing phone, a buzzing doorbell. Certain activities, however, don't call to us so loudly. Yet, these can have an impact more profound than all the others combined: activities such as walking in a park, visiting relatives, tossing a baseball . . . or building a Lego city. These are the experiences that build up a soul.

What would happen if, today, all parents made their children their top priority? Nowadays, we often complain about teenagers and their lack of respect for adults, and we worry about the anger and lack of direction that seem to plague them to the point of violence; yet, I meet many parents who tell me that *their* teenagers are wonderful young people and that they enjoy their children now, *just as they always have.* Therein lies a lesson: We need to begin, right now, to see each second as a gift, as an opportunity to savor where we all are *now*—whether we do this by playing, conversing, or simply being together with our children. In so doing, we may weave a lifeline that continues to hold throughout the years. When that Lego city gets built, so does the foundation to a future. And a minute of time for a child will someday be worth its equivalent in hours to the adult she becomes. The time we spend with our children at this very moment—nurturing, teaching, and loving them—is the substance that helps mold them into the people that they will become.

Changes You Can Make

Review the priorities in your life, make a list of your top five, and begin investing the bulk of your time and energy in those choices. If you are a parent, your list—of course—should include your children. Keep your list of five handy, and refer to it whenever a decision arises. Ask yourself, "Does what I am doing, or about to do, fit into my list of priorities?"

Unlike much advice, this way of living is not "easier said than done." On the contrary, it's "easier done than said"! You'll often be surprised to discover that it doesn't take hours to satisfy a child's need for attention. Sometimes fifteen minutes of undivided attention will fill your child's cup—and then allow you to tend to your daily rituals without that nagging sense of guilt, or that feeling that something essential is missing. In the story of Jeff and Lily, if he had dropped everything upon his arrival at home and given Lily thirty minutes of undivided attention, he might have fulfilled her need for his love. She might then have been happy to scamper off and allow him to get to his business, or perhaps trailed along with him, letting their connection linger through the evening.

Of course, some daily tasks must be done regardless of their placement on your list. The laundry would definitely not be in my top five, but it still needs to be done! However, your list will help ensure that these "maintenance" tasks are done with the proper acknowledgment of their importance. This means that I may decide that a game of Monopoly with my children is worth postponing the laundry until after they've gone to bed.

As for those must-do tasks, some can be undertaken with a child included as helper or as company—a three-year-old can sit beside you with her plastic kitchen set, "preparing" her own dinner, as you prepare dinner for the family; a five-year-old can sort socks or fold hand towels as you fold the rest of the laundry; a seven-year-old can accompany you on your round of errands. In each case, you will very likely enjoy the time talking together.

When you decree that your family and your children are your priority, and that you want, and need, to spend more time with them, your daily decisions will become easier. You may even begin to ascertain that some goals you had rated as "top priority" are supremely unimportant. And as a natural and direct effect, these will fall away, leaving you with two undeniable gains: a heightened and refined sense of values, and the freedom to pursue them.

Zoo Day

Melissa woke up after a perfect night's sleep feeling refreshed and energetic. The sun shining through the window added yet more joy to this beautiful spring day. As she sprang out of bed, a thought hit her, and she began to giggle like a schoolgirl. What a wonderful day to play hooky! An idea began to take shape. She'd never done anything like this before, but, after all, what was life for? Yes!, she thought, I'll take a personal day off of work, actually let the boys skip school, and the three of us will spend this glorious day at the zoo! As she got dressed, she added up her reasons to validate this slightly naughty endeavor: she'd get to spend some quality time with the boys, they'd get to enjoy a day with each other, and they'd all have a respite from the rigors of their daily routine. She warmed to her vision of the three of them laughing and strolling through the zoo, the boys jabbering together and gushing their appreciation for their fabulous day and their hip mom.

She bustled off to wake up her kids and share her pleasant surprise. She bounded into Kevin's room first and sat beside him on the bed. "Ok, sleepyhead! Time to get up." The answer was a groan from under the covers.

Next was Luke's room. She rolled his wheelchair beside the bed and suggested he choose shorts and a T-shirt for this fine temperate day. She almost blurted out her plans but thought better of it: she decided to get the kids up and dressed before telling them.

As the boys ate breakfast, Melissa sat at the table across from them. Fairly bursting with her idea, she blurted, "How'd you guys like to skip school today? I thought we'd play hooky and head to the zoo!" Her eyes wide with excitement, she waited for their expressions of glee.

Luke looked mildly pleased but definitely not enraptured. Kevin scrunched up his face and wrinkled his nose. "The *zoo*? I don't want to go to the *zoo*," he moaned.

Melissa was a little disappointed, but she just *knew* they'd have a great time once they got there. "Oh, come *on*," she said, "we'll have a ball!"

Kevin looked doubtful. "Who has fun at the *zoo*?"

She wasn't about to give up on her wonderful plan, but her short-tempered response sounded like a bursting balloon. "We're going to the *zoo*, and you're going to have *fun*. It's a *sunny* day, I've already called in for the day *off*, and this is *quality time* with your mother."

Kevin and Luke just stared at their mom. "Yeah, yeah," said Kevin. "Let's go to the zoo. Whoopee."

Determined not to let this little setback ruin her plans, Melissa gathered up their stuff and herded the boys into the van. Once she'd folded and loaded Luke's chair, she hopped into the front seat with a broad grin on her face. "Here we go!" She didn't see the looks her boys shot each other behind her.

They weren't even out of the neighborhood when Luke's voice pierced Melissa's cheerful mood. "Mom! Kevin took my markers!"

"Did not," Kevin retorted. "They're mine!"

"Are not!" yelled Luke. "Make him give 'em back!"

"Boys!" growled Melissa. "You're not even supposed to have markers in the van. Give them to me." Melissa waved her hand backward over the seat, motioning for the markers.

"Well, if they're *yours*, then *you* give her the markers," Kevin sneered at his brother.

"I can't reach. You do it."

"No. Figure it out."

Melissa snapped her fingers. "Just *give* me the markers," she growled.

They rode down the street in relative silence for the next fifteen minutes. Melissa turned on the radio and began to sing along. Her cheerful mood was returning.

When they arrived at the zoo, the handicapped spots were full—with cars that didn't belong there, of course—so Melissa had to drive around the enormous lot twice before finding a spot. After unloading the chair, their gear, and themselves, they proceeded toward the zoo entrance. It wasn't until they were nearly at the gate—and the steep flight of stone stairs—that she spied the Wheelchair Access sign, with its arrow pointing to the opposite side of the lot. In frustrated silence, they trudged back to the van and reloaded, only to repeat the process at the opposite side of the lot. As they approached the promised entrance, Luke piped up, "Kevin's right. This isn't gonna be any fun at all."

Melissa didn't even have the energy to answer. She paid for their tickets, expressed her complaint about the inappropriately filled handicapped parking spots, and ushered the boys through the large iron gates. "Where do you want to go first?" she asked.

"Let's go see the lions and tigers," Kevin suggested.

"No way! I wanna see the elephants and giraffes," protested Luke.

"Why do we always have to do what you want?" complained Kevin. "I vote for the lions and tigers."

Melissa pulled the plug on the argument. "We'll go to the reptile house." She stated it firmly and stomped away, both boys groaning as they followed.

Melissa was enjoying the reptile house until she turned to see Kevin pushing Luke through the halls, nearly knocking over a woman and her baby as they popped wheelchair wheelies. Her clenched teeth were all that stood between a controlled but angry reprimand and a loud, angry outburst.

The disgruntled trio headed to the African Jungle. On the way there they passed a cotton candy stand. Oh, what the heck,

Melissa thought. Cotton candy before lunch—why not? "Wait here a sec," she said to the boys. But her big sweet surprise brought nothing but more complaints.

"Why'd you get *pink*?" complained Luke.

"How come only *one*?" Kevin whined. "I suppose Luke gets to hold it!"

"Well, if *you* hold it, nobody else will get to eat any, since you're such a *pig*!"

"Knock it off!" yelled Melissa, on the verge of tears. "This is supposed to be fun!"

Kevin smirked at her. "Well, I *told* you the zoo wasn't any fun."

Melissa whirled Luke around so fast that he lost his balance. "Come on," she growled at Kevin, who had to run to catch up.

"What are you doing?" Luke asked her.

"I have a headache," Melissa responded. "We're going home."

The boys cried all the way back, while Melissa held her aching head and fumed over a totally wasted day.

The Hidden Message

"My expectations are so far from reality that the only possible result is my disappointment and anger."

Think About It

Expectations: our lives are full of them. On the day the pregnancy test reads positive, we begin contemplating beautiful rosy vignettes of what our lives as parents will be like; it's Mother Nature's way of fostering parent-child bonds and the hope that keeps us going. As our children grow, we continue to envision how we hope things will turn out. We set up ideals—some realistic, some not. Eventually, the former delight us, and the latter . . . sometimes they break our hearts.

A mother discovers that her robust newborn will never run on a baseball field, or even walk to school, and that they will face problems that she never even knew existed. The parents of three girls hope the birth of number four will add some variety to the family makeup, only to discover that they will have plenty of use for the pink frilly dresses packed in the attic. A father, himself an only child, anticipates a close and loving relationship between the twins his wife is expecting—only to find that daily bickering and fighting between them are more common than friendship. A mother who has a close and loving relationship with her daughter turns around one day to ask who this sullen, selfish, moody, and demanding teenager living with her is.

Our great expectations frame the big picture as well as the innumerable small close-ups of our daily lives. We project countless idealized scenarios for our every day: the little one will behave in church; the painstakingly planned birthday party will be a smash; the new puppy will fit into the family perfectly . . . the outing at the zoo will be perfect. It's a fact of life: many of these small conceptions are destined for failure.

The difference between expectation and reality equals unhappiness. The more specific and lofty our expectations, the harder we fall when reality crashes down on us.

Changes You Can Make

Take a good look at your own expectations for your children and your life. Examine them and determine if they are realistic and likely. Don't be afraid to make an honest assessment of where you are, how this status compares with what you know to be "typical," and where you think you may be pointed. Then make adjustments in your expectations so that they more closely match reality.

One way of making this exercise work is to become more knowledgeable about the stages of child development. When you are familiar with typical patterns of childhood—and there are many—you have a benchmark against which to measure the issues that arise daily. The vast bodies of research and observation available to you can help you see when your child's behavior is usual for his age and situation, and when it is outside the norm and requires more attention. For example, if a mom with a selfish and demanding teenage daughter were well read about what to expect in adolescence, she wouldn't feel responsible for her daughter's behavioral changes. She would know that, no matter how close and loving the relationship with parents, nearly all teenagers endure hormonal and emotional upheaval at this time in their lives.

I am by no means suggesting pessimism, and in fact, realistic expectations *prevent* pessimism. The more realistic your expectations, the more possible it is to raise your children with optimism. In other words, when your expectations are realistic enough, your children's success is at least possible, and you will feel successful as a parent. When expectations are extreme and unrealistic, then failure is the most likely result. As an example, if you have more than one child, and you expect that they will never bicker, never fight, and always be cheerful best of friends, you are setting yourself up for disappointment and anger.

On the flip side, I'm not proposing that you passively accept "typical" misbehavior just because you expected it! Understanding and accepting your child's behavior in a realistic way can help you isolate areas that may require your attention, or may act as a warning light telling you that the situation requires taking the time to explore various solutions. So, when you understand that siblings will bicker and fight, sometimes just as often as they are cheerful best of friends (and sometimes, more!), you can relax with the knowledge that your kids are behaving normally—and then explore the many ways in which you can encourage a more positive relationship between them. As another example, if your child doesn't tolerate transitions well, it doesn't mean that you have to live your life on a rigid schedule—it means that you need to be creative in helping your child learn to cope.

Another advantage to having down-to-earth designs is that you can often modify events in your life to *prevent* some of the problems that you foresee. So, instead of fighting against what you *know* will happen, you institute changes to keep the situation from occurring in the first place. In our story, Melissa, blinded perhaps by her own excitement, rejected the evidence that neither son was very keen on the zoo's being the day's destination. Maybe if she had offered them an opportunity to help plan the outing, they would have been in a better frame of mind.

Here are a few examples that illustrate this same point: If you know that your toddler gets fussy when you plan several errands in a row, you might try to rearrange your day to include lunch in the park midway through your roster of stops. If you know that your preteen daughter is fussy about what she wears, then take her shopping with you to allow her to help choose what you buy. If your two children have been playing nicely for the past hour, and you suspect that the sudden bickering that you hear is about to escalate into a vocal war, then intercept them with an invitation to bake cookies or join you in a different activity.

When you hold fast to realistic expectations, life won't throw you for as many loops. When you use your insight about expectations to make good decisions, you can approach this momentous job we call parenting with a calm demeanor and a level head—and enjoy more happy endings.

Peaceful Saturday?

Anne woke slowly and stretched. She loved Saturdays—the leisurely pace after a hectic week of work and school activities. Extra time with her daughters, Jessica and Laura. Freedom to run errands unfettered by other obligations.

She dressed and made her way leisurely down the stairs. The first sound that met her was the annoying screech of TV cartoon characters. She poked her head into the family room. "Girls! Shut off the TV! You know I don't want you starting the day in front of the tube."

"But, Mom. This is our favorite show. Can we turn it off when it's over?"

"No," answered Anne. "You know the rule: no TV before breakfast. Turn it off *now*." She then noticed that the girls were still in their pajamas. "And you're not even dressed yet! Go on back upstairs and get dressed—then have some breakfast."

The girls did as they were told and clambered upstairs to change their clothes. A while later, wondering what was taking so long, Anne called up to them, "Girls!" No response. Halfway up the stairs, Anne saw that their bedroom door was shut; behind it emanated hushed giggles and radio music. She trudged the rest of the way up the stairs and opened the door. "Jessica and Laura. You need to keep this door open so you can hear me when I call you. How many times do I have to tell you that? It's tiring to have to come all the way up here like this." She sighed, appraising the daughters who stood frozen in mid-dance in the center of the room. The sisters passed a resigned look between them that their mother missed. The look said it was going to be one of those mornings.

"Geez! You're not even dressed yet. Would you girls *please* get dressed and come down for breakfast?" Anne turned to go back down to the kitchen, leaving a cloud of admonitions, complaints, and negative observations about her daughters' behavior hanging in the air. The girls barely heard her mumbling, although it continued right down into the kitchen.

As Anne ate the breakfast she'd made for herself, she bristled at the sound of the girls' footsteps thumping down the stairs. Why couldn't they walk more softly? As if in response, the footsteps stopped. She waited. Then she heard the girls' voices coming from the front hall. She wandered over to see them sitting on the floor sorting through their rock collections. "Come on, girls, breakfast time," Anne reminded them.

"But, Mom, we're not hungry yet," answered Jessica.

"Honey, it's almost 10:00. I'd like you to eat something."

Laura piped in, "Can we just finish sorting?"

Anne huffed, "Why do you girls always push me? Just eat breakfast. *Now.*"

The girls scooped up their rocks and followed Anne into the kitchen. They reached into the cabinet at the same time, grabbing for the same cereal bowl. The pile of bowls clattered to the counter in a culinary avalanche. The girls would have let loose a giggle if Anne hadn't looked up with obvious annoyance. "Be more careful," she grumbled.

Their bowls recovered and filled with cereal and milk, the girls took their places at the table. Anne frowned as Laura left a trail of milk in her wake. "Laura!" Anne chided. "You're making a mess! I keep telling you not to put so much milk in your bowl." Anne scraped her chair away from the table, snatched up a sponge, and huffily wiped up the mess. By the time she'd finished, the girls had resumed their rock sorting in the family room . . . but not for long.

Anne tensed when she noticed the open cereal boxes on the counter, flanked by the dirty bowls and a fair spattering of milk all over the table. The constant mess! Anne finally snapped. "Laura! Jessica! Get in here and clean off the table! And put the cereal away—if you leave it open like this, it just gets stale. You are not babies! I expect you to clean up after yourselves!"

The lovely Saturday morning Anne had anticipated was going sour, right along with the milk splotches on the counter. She sighed long and deep, wondering why it seemed that *all* her Saturday mornings were curdling lately.

The Hidden Message

"Not one little mistake, not one little accident, not one tiny mishap will slip by me unnoticed or uncorrected. You are not children; you are miniature adults, subject to the same standards and expectations as adults. Adults at their best, no less."

Think About It

In his wonderful book *Don't Sweat the Small Stuff with Your Family* (Hyperion, 1998), Richard Carlson tells this story: "I was speaking at a bookstore to a crowd of people when someone asked me an interesting question: 'How would you describe the average person in two words or less?' After reflecting for a moment, I answered, 'Easily bothered.' The entire room burst into laughter because everyone recognized that I had hit on an almost universal truth—most of us are bothered by practically everything."

When raising children this is especially true. Why? Let's consider what we want as parents. We want to be good parents. We want to take our job as teachers seriously and strive to do the best we can. We don't want to miss a single opportunity to help our children learn something about life; at times, it seems that we want every moment to be a "teaching moment." We want our children to be well behaved and to develop into great people. And while we're overseeing all this, we want our days to be peaceful and happy.

These are all honorable goals. And we need to stay focused on them. However, at times—maybe when we become a little shaky in our opinions of ourselves as parents, or when we compare our children and our parenting habits with those of others, or when some event causes us to "raise the bar" on our standards for acceptable behavior—we become "nitpickers." We go overboard and drive ourselves and our children crazy by becoming Behavior Cops.

You certainly need to take your job as a parent seriously. However, if you find yourself nagging and complaining from sunup to sundown, you might need to be choosier in picking your battles. And make no mistake: it's difficult to ascertain whether you're on target or overshooting. Families are as unique as the children who compose them, and the boundary between reasonable correction and flat-out nagging is different for each.

Changes You Can Make

So, how do you know where that boundary is? As in so many other situations in parenting, I'd suggest you go with your gut. If you pay close enough attention to what you say, how you say it, and when you say it, you might uncover clues to your motivations. Trust yourself. Or, failing that, trust your children. Watch how they react when you communicate with them. You may (or you may not) find the boundary in their eyes. Being aware that the unreasonable behavior may sometimes be *yours* is liberating. Maybe your kids aren't so bad after all!

Remember that there's no such thing as a kid (or adult, for that matter) who behaves maturely, responsibly, and perfectly 100 percent of the time. Children spill, forget, dally, yell, disrupt, explode, implode, whine, demand, squabble, procrastinate, and snivel. Children are so . . . *childish.* So wonderfully, delightfully, *appropriately* childish. Sometimes all it takes to smooth things out is to realign our expectations and make them more realistic for the child, his abilities, his disposition, and his age. For instance, if a parent were to complain that her fourteen-year-old is acting a bit rebellious, it would help her to remember that this is what fourteen-year-olds *do*. Bearing this trait in mind, she'll not be so "easily bothered"—and can help the child best channel these normal, appropriate breakaway urges with a clearer head. She can operate from a position of strength, rather than weakness borne of burnout.

After I'd given a lecture one evening, a mother asked for my advice. Her two-year-old was constantly annoying her by getting into everything, not listening to her, and always testing her tolerance. Trying to lighten up this mother's mood, I suggested that, when she became annoyed, she should tell her two-year-old these three things: "Grow up!" "Act your age!" "Don't be such a baby!" We both laughed. Because, obviously, her child *was* in the process of growing up, was acting her age in spades, and *was* still a baby!

So, begin by examining your expectations and making sure they're appropriate. Once you do that, continue lowering your blood pressure by deciding to choose your battles wisely. Let the little stuff slide, and conserve your energy for the major ruptures. A few qualifying questions can help you gauge the crisis level: "What impact will this *one thing* have on my child's development? Is it a pattern, or just a random occurrence? Is it causing harm to anyone? Just how important is this?"

Also remember: what you deem important may differ from what your neighbor, your parents, and your friends suggest. Follow your heart. Taking into account everything you know of your child, weigh his or her abilities against the accepted standard, and decide if the actions need correction—or if they are inconsequential in the grand scheme of things.

In our story, Anne started out reveling in the fact that it was Saturday, a day of leisure. From the beginning, she had great expectations. And the peace and quiet of this Saturday depended on her kids' not acting like . . . well, kids. All these expectations piled up and buried her when they clashed with reality, and she acted out her disappointment and frustration by turning into the Behavior Cop. She was so stressed out about their recalcitrance in turning off the TV, getting dressed, and having breakfast—and for what? If it's a morning of leisure—for all of them—what would be the harm in allowing them to proceed at a slug's pace? Why not let them watch their favorite show, stay in their pj's a while longer, eat a bit later? After all, they were having a fun time together—and as any parent of more than one child knows, that's time to be treasured. What, in the broader view, was so harmful?

Anne also worked herself up over the bowls dropping to the counter, the milk spilling onto the floor, the cleanup that was not executed immediately and correctly (haven't we all?). But these are all typical childish behaviors. Yes, they need to be corrected—but perhaps not in such an abrasive manner. When children hear negative comments as a rule, they quickly learn to tune them out. And when we've lost their ears, we risk losing the children themselves, eventually.

When the girls were so eager to sort their rock collections, what would have been the harm in Anne's sitting down *with* them, letting them tell her what was so interesting about those rocks that they absolutely, positively had to look at them before breakfast? Perhaps it would even allow Anne to absorb some of their childish happiness—since children rarely are afflicted with the "easily bothered" syndrome. (And if you do have one of those children who *are* "easily bothered," changing your own patterns could provide a healthy role model from whom your child can learn.)

Becoming less "easily bothered" takes effort. But it brings many wonderful benefits. First, by consciously questioning the practical implications of each misstep you're tempted to instruct upon or nag about, you'll be able to choose the important ones. Did you read that carefully? "Choose." It's all up to you—you don't have to always respond negatively if you separate the trip-ups from the nosedives. And when you do this, your words on the issues that *do* matter won't be lost upon your children in a ceaseless stream of corrections. Because they'll learn that you react strongly only when it matters, they'll be more likely to *hear* you when you do make those corrections.

If you learn to let the little things go, you'll enjoy your kids more. They will enjoy *you* more. You'll be more relaxed, and you'll have more fun. You'll be less stressed and less irritated. You will begin to react to life's little nudges much less and to enjoy your own life much more. And a little parenting magic just might occur after all, in the kind of "teaching moments" that happen when parents and children are together in a relaxed and peaceful setting.

8

Messages About Parenting Styles

When You Wish upon a Star

For the third time that morning, Shaeida stood in her daughter's room, trying to wake her up. "Nikki! Honey! It's getting late; you should be up already." Nikki groaned and moved a bit but made no attempt to rise. Shaeida opened the drapes and began pulling her sleepy daughter's clothes from the closet, and taking umbrage at the usual mess Nikki had made of freshly laundered and folded piles. "Nikki! Why don't you keep your things folded up neatly? It's frustrating for me to keep tidying up after you. Come on! It's after 7:00. We'll be late if you don't get up . . ."

At long last, Nikki joined her mother for breakfast—or something vaguely similar to it. Shaeida glanced up from her newspaper to comment. "I don't think you can call brownies a healthy breakfast . . ." Nikki shrugged and held up her nutritious glass of milk, which was the most reassurance she could muster for her mother.

All of a sudden, Nikki jumped up as if stuck by a pin. "Oh *no*," she moaned. "I didn't finish my spelling homework! Where is it?" As she darted about, gathering her schoolwork, her mother looked up in exasperation.

"You're in fifth grade now; it would be nice if you developed some good homework routines. I really think you should get in the habit of finishing your homework when you get home from school. When you save it for the end of the day, you always seem to forget something."

"Oh, Mom," Nikki scoffed, "it's not a big deal. Don't be such a nag. I'll finish everything."

Shaeida stood and banged her coffee cup on the table. "It would be nice if you could find your manners, young lady!"

"Sorry," Nikki replied distractedly to her mom, who by now was standing near the door, rattling her car keys. Nikki didn't notice; she was preoccupied with the hem of her pants. "Hold on. These pants are too short. I need to change."

"Honey, just wear what you have on, OK? We have to go."

"Mom, I'll be really quick."

Shaeida glanced at the clock, which insisted that they should have been out the door five minutes ago. She called up the stairs, "I really wish you'd hurry! We're going to be late!"

The Hidden Message

"If it's not too much trouble, and if the timing is right, and if it's OK with you, would you mind very much doing what I ask? Oh, I *really* wish you would, but if not, that's OK. I won't get too pushy about it."

Think About It

"You should . . ." "Why don't you . . ." "I don't think . . ." "It would be nice . . ." "I really wish you'd . . ." ". . . OK?" Parents who get in the habit of using these "wishing" statements are often frustrated and confused as to why their children don't listen to them. The reason is that all these phrases are noncommittal. They are suggestions, not imperatives. And so, the child interprets the directives as a "wish list"––gently proffered ideas that can be accepted or rejected as the child desires.

Not convinced? These phrases are just mannerly, you say? Then, take a look at some perfectly logical responses to these typical "wishing" messages:

Parent's Wish	**Child's Response**
"You should . . ."	"Maybe, but I don't think I will."
"Why don't you . . ."	"Because I don't want to."
"I don't think . . ."	"Really? But I think something different."
"It would be nice . . ."	"I suppose it would. But I'm still not going to."
"I really wish you would . . ."	"That's nice to know."
"Ok? . . ."	"Umm, no. Since you asked."

Changes You Can Make

Purge all these wishing statements from your vocabulary. You are the parent. It is your job, your right, and your responsibility to see that your child does the deeds that need to be done and that she behaves appropriately. To do all this with facility, you and your child must maintain a hierarchy of command. And you are at the top. Elevating your child's position to yours may make her like you for the moment, but it does her no favors in the long run. And these wishy-washy phrases are the stool on which your child perches to get up there to your level. (It's much better to let children grow into the job.)

Don't ever imply that obedience is an option. But this doesn't mean dispensing with courtesy. (After all, it's ridiculous to demand respect from someone whom you treat with none.) Just use this simple formula to compose your requests: "please" + [insert task here]. It's that easy—and effective, as long as you're prepared to follow through with requisite consequences in cases of nonperformance. See how much more "in charge" Shaeida could sound, while being polite and specific with her requests:

"Please get up and get dressed right now so that we can leave on time."

"Please keep your clothes folded neatly."

"Please put the brownie away and eat something more nutritious for breakfast."

"Please do your homework when you get home."

"Please speak to me with respect."

"Please wear what you have on."

Another option is offering your child a choice that allows her some control over her actions within limits that you set. Using choice is a wonderful parenting tool. It can be used in many ways. An either-or choice: "You may have either cereal or waffles. You choose." A sequence choice: "What do you want to do first, your homework or the dishes?" A time choice: "Do you want to start your project now or wait until 7:00?" Multiple choice: "Do you want to wear your coat, carry it, or put on a sweatshirt?"

A when-then statement is another positive way to express your requirements. Tell your child what she *needs* to do before moving on to what she *wants* to do. "When your clothes are neatly folded, then I will do the rest of your laundry." A when-then proposition like this one, which awards you the final action, gives your child the power to bring about a certain result, while you maintain control.

One more suggestion: create specific rules to govern everyday situations. Once you have articulated what your rules are, be relentless in requiring consistent compliance. After a time, they will become habit, and your life will be all the easier. "Nikki, the new rule around here is that, immediately after school, you will sit at the table and do your homework." You can even follow it up with a when-then statement: "When your homework is done, then you may do what you'd like with the rest of your afternoon until dinner."

These approaches allow the parent to retain control and to communicate direct and clear expectations. In addition, if your child does not do as you ask, and your requests are specific and easily understood, you know that your child's noncooperation demonstrates disobedience, not misunderstanding.

From the child's perspective, a no-nonsense, obedience-is-no-option request leads her to do what you want rather than implying that she can create her own agenda.

My Kid, the Lawyer Wannabe

She opened with a question. "Mom! What are we having for dinner?"

"Well, hello to you, *too*, honey," Judy said with a chuckle, leaning over to press a kiss on Jennifer's cheek. "We're having fish."

"What kind?" asked Jennifer, chin raised in suspicion.

"Cod," warily answered Judy. She knew the prosecution would begin straightaway.

Jennifer peered down her nose into the pan. "And how are you making it?" she inquired.

"I'm baking it. With lemon and seasoning," Judy replied, trying to sound nonchalant about her gourmet cooking skills.

"But, *Mom*." Jennifer's voice reflected the grimace on her face. "You know I *hate* it that way! . . . Don't you?"

Judy had to admit: the kid was good. But Judy held her own, patiently explaining that it was the family's favorite. To which Jennifer responded, "But why can't you just bread a few pieces for me?"

"Because," Judy began, "it takes too much time and effort for the one small piece you'll manage to eat." Motion denied.

"Well, it can't be that difficult!" wailed Jennifer. "Why don't you just . . ."

"Jennifer! Stop with the fish already!" Judy interrupted. "It's garbage day. Please collect the trash and take it out while I'm making dinner."

"Why do I have to do it every time?" huffed Jennifer.

"It's your *job*," Judy countered over her objections.

"But it's been my job forever," pleaded Jennifer. "I don't see why Jason can't do it."

Judy calmly listed Jason's jobs and explained that he, too, had responsibilities.

Jennifer was not appeased by the defense presented on Jason's behalf. "Taking out the garbage for the whole family is just asking too much. It's smelly and heavy and *icky*. I'd much rather sweep the kitchen floor. I think it's time that we switched jobs."

"I'll think about it," responded Judy distractedly, her fatigued head taking a little unscheduled adjournment.

"Well, why can't you think about it right now?" hammered Jennifer.

"Because I'm making *dinner* right now."

"So, you can't make dinner and think at the same time?"

Judy closed her eyes, her hands going limp on the counter. Objection! She paused to restore order in the court that had taken over her kitchen, then looked over at Jennifer. "Will you just take out the trash and let me make dinner?"

"But you didn't answer me! Why can't we talk about this now?"

"Jennifer, please. Just do it."

Jennifer, never ready to concede a case, shouted, "I'm sick and tired of taking out the garbage!"

Judy, her patience at its end, yelled back, "I don't care! Just do the job!"

Jennifer's volume also increasing, she bellowed, "I don't want to!"

Judy slammed down the spoon she'd been holding. "I don't care what you want, young lady! Take that trash out!"

Jennifer recognized her mother's danger zone and knew she'd be held in contempt soon if she didn't back off. She yanked the kitchen trash (into which Judy was still tossing fish remnants) and stomped out of the kitchen, mumbling something about a dictatorship and unfairness.

The Hidden Message

"It takes two to argue, and I'm ready whenever you are!"

Think About It

If you have a child like Jennifer, and you're constantly frustrated with her, it's time for an exercise that a wise old teacher once prescribed: Point your index finger in the classic way, and check out the three fingers now pointing back at *you*. In other words, you need to acknowledge and take responsibility for your own argumentative behavior before you attempt to correct your child's. Every time you rationalize, explain, and bicker with a child who is willing to deliberate every point, you give her more and more leeway in which to plead her case.

Apply the question a famous philosopher posed long ago—the one that begins, "If a tree falls in a forest . . ."—to Judy's situation. If a tree argues with another tree that doesn't argue back, is there indeed an argument?

Changes You Can Make

If you really want your child to stop arguing with you, give her less feedback when she begins her dispute process. Shut it right down by stating your case in a firm, authoritative manner—and then being quiet. Ignore the ensuing argumentative comments, or simply repeat your original request. If you're too tempted to argue back, walk away for a few minutes and promise yourself that you won't let this goading turn into a two-way argument. Teach your child that your word is final. Realize that, when you do this, your very vocal child will *have* to complain a bit. But when you fail to take up the gauntlet, these arguments turn into harmless mumbling.

A different option is to change the tiring process of "arguing" into a more productive mode of "debating." The principle here is to adopt and abide by the standard rules for formal debate. Some children enjoy the give-and-take of a debate, and you can encourage this intellectual exchange of thoughts—which is healthy and instructive in the right context—by setting limits. Let your child know which issues can and can't be debated. Have a standard reply for a nonnegotiable issue, such as "This is not open for discussion." Let her know that raising of voices, name-calling, or rude comments will not be accepted or acknowledged, and that each party must be given time to explain a point of view without interruption. To help her understand that these are universally accepted bylaws, show her books that instruct in the fine art of debate. Explain that debating is an extracurricular activity in many schools and that a well-established set of rules governs the procedure. Amaze her with the fact that many perfectly sane people pay vast sums of money to learn the intricacies of the art—in law school. Be sure, however, to emphasize how the process employed between parent and child differs from a standard court. In the High Court of Home, you are Supreme Court Judge—and you decide which subjects can be debated and which cannot, when an argument is concluded, and what the final decision will be, regardless of her finesse in the forum.

One parenting skill that every parent of a lawyer wannabe would be wise to master, and use often, is offering choices instead of issuing commands. Kids with a ready answer to every statement often do very well when given a choice. In this story, if Judy had revised her command "Take out the trash while I'm making dinner" into a choice—"Would you like to take out the trash now or after we eat?"—Jennifer may well have done the job without complaint, since she has been given some control over her destiny. (If Jennifer concludes that she doesn't want to do either, Judy can just smile and respond, "That wasn't one of the choices. Now or after dinner?")

Another way to reduce the number of cases that your lawyer wannabe takes on is to implement fixed routines in your home. For example, if kitchen cleanup and trash removal transpire immediately after the last bite of food is consumed at the table, and homework is done immediately after cleanup, then your child will develop concrete habits that leave less room for contention.

The desire to argue with a parent has its roots in the eternal childhood quest for power. And if your child can provoke a spirited response from you, and open the floor for an argument between equal parties, she knows she has the power. You can take it away by implementing the procedures described here. Or you can choose to control how *much* power she has by setting limits to your debate or by giving her choices; this allows her the sense of control she's after, while allowing you to retain a firm grip on the gavel.

Dog Doo To-Do

"Dad! I'm home!" Melody announced her arrival from school in the typical way. "Where are you?"

"In my office, Mel," Kevin answered. She ambled in, knowing she'd get a hug, a smile, and an inquiry about her day. After they exchanged greetings and Melody told him about her day at school, she turned to leave the room. Kevin stopped her. "Mel? Before you go out to play, would you mind picking up the dog doo in the yard? You know you're supposed to do it in the morning before you leave."

Melody wrinkled her nose. "Sorry, Daddy. I forgot. I'll do it."

A while later, Kevin finished his work. As he entered the kitchen to start dinner, he spotted Melody out on the swing set. He also spotted the various brown lumps decorating his lawn. Kevin opened the window and called out to remind his daughter, "Melody! Don't forget to pick up the dog doo!"

"Ok!" she answered back cheerfully.

Soon after, Kevin called Melody for dinner. "What do you say we eat outside? It's really nice out." As the two of them toted their food out to the picnic table, Kevin had to sidestep several doggie deposits. "Mel, this is really gross. I wish you'd get it picked up."

"I'll do it right after dinner. Promise." Melody looked contrite, but her dad looked unconvinced.

Dad and daughter enjoyed a pleasant dinner, despite the canine ambiance, catching up on the latest news and tossing around ideas for the upcoming weekend. As soon as they'd cleared the picnic table and tidied up the kitchen, Melody gathered up her homework and began studying diligently for her math test.

Kevin put his hand on her shoulder. "Honey . . . I'm really proud of you for being so conscientious about your homework . . . but are you *ever* going to pick up that dog doo?"

The Hidden Message

"If you can put up with the drone of my voice, go ahead and feel free to ignore me. I don't plan to take any action about this issue at all."

Think About It

An inescapable part of parenting is getting our children to do many things they'd rather not, like picking up dog doo, taking out trash, cleaning their rooms, and finishing homework. When a parent continues to remind, ask, beg, pester, and yes, nag a child about a task, but fails to follow through with any action, the parent actually gives the child an interesting choice: either listen to the nagging, or do the task. The child is free to decide that the minimal pain of listening to a parent beg over and over is a small price to pay for sidestepping the dreaded deed. And children often do make that choice, sometimes without realizing it.

All of Kevin's comments to Melody are vague, and without any follow-through action on his part, he may as well say, "If you could manage to pick up the dog doo sometime before your next birthday, that would be really nice."

Changes You Can Make

You can avoid slipping into the nagging trap. Simply follow this four-step process: (1) think, (2) tell, (3) warn, (4) act.

1. **Think.** Before you ask your child to do something, think about exactly *what* you want, *when* you want it done, and *how* your child should proceed. Be clear about your purpose.

2. **Tell.** Once you're certain about what you want, tell your child. Avoid any phrase that makes your request sound optional. Be specific. For example, "Melody, I would like the dog doo picked up before we sit down to dinner at 6:00."

3. **Warn.** If the deadline looms and the requested task has not been completed, let your child know that you are aware of this, and remind her to get the job done. "Melody, dinner will be ready in ten minutes. You are to pick up the dog doo before we eat."

4. **Act.** If the deadline has been reached and the task has not been performed, you have a wide variety of options that all come under the heading "act."

   - You could nudge your child in the right direction with physical help. (Put the shovel and bucket in her hand, and guide her out to the yard.)

   - You could use a when-then statement. ("Melody, I'll be eating my dinner in the kitchen. When you have picked up the dog doo, then you may join me.")

   - You might follow through with a consequence. ("Melody, since you didn't do as I asked, you'll be staying home after dinner instead of going to your friend's house as you had planned.)

   - If this is a repeat offense, you might invite your child to sit down for a heart-to-heart. Express your displeasure and your expectation. Brainstorm a solution. For example, you may decide that she needs to create a checklist and keep it posted in a prominent place, such as on the front of the refrigerator, so that she'll remember to do her chore each day. Then hand her a piece of paper, a ruler, and a box of markers and ask her to create the list then and there.

- You might choose to do it yourself. I know, I know—you're thinking, "What!?!" But wait, you didn't let me finish. Do it yourself, and let her know which of *your* jobs she can do for you. ("It's 6:00, and since you did not pick up the dog doo, I took the time to do it for you. Which means that, in return, you'll take the time to pull the weeds for me after dinner.")

Keep in mind that, if you already have demonstrated a gift for "gentle reminding, asking, nagging, and hinting," it will take some time to convince your child that you have changed. And she'll get the hint that you mean business only if you're consistent in employing the last step ("act"). If you repeat step 3 ("warn"), twice, three times, a dozen times . . . you defeat the process and default into your former Nag Mode.

Perfect Kids

Hank pulled into the driveway of his home at precisely 5:35, as he did every weekday. He snatched his briefcase from the seat and walked briskly toward the house. As he entered his domain, he smiled to find his four children exactly where they were expected to be every day at this time: at the kitchen table doing their homework. One at a time, they looked up and greeted their dad. He rounded the table and ruffled each child's hair, then grabbed his newspaper, which was sitting (as it should be) on the edge of the counter. He segued over to his recliner to catch up on the day's news, pleased with his obviously advanced parenting skills. You know Hank; everybody does. He's the one who always smiles smugly whenever conversation turns to strategies for dealing with child-rearing challenges, for he knows that *he* has a handle on things in his home; he doesn't need any blather about the latest *strategies*.

The telephone rang, and his fifteen-year-old daughter, Shauna, popped up to answer it. Hank looked over the top edge of his glasses and his newspaper. He halted her route to the phone with a question. "And is your homework done, young lady?"

"No, Dad," she answered meekly. With one longing glance at the telephone, she morosely listened to her friend leave a message on the machine as she returned to the table to finish her work. Hank returned to his paper, glad there was no (what he termed) New Age walk-all-over-the-parents stuff in *this* house.

As Shauna was taking her place at the table, her twelve-year-old sister, Rachel, amused herself by wrapping a foot around the edge of Shauna's chair and tugging at it—until Shauna landed none too delicately on the floor. Rachel laughed, Shauna hissed, and both swallowed hard when they looked up to see Hank striding toward the table and wearing his sternest face. "*This* is homework time, and I'll *not* have the shenanigans. Rachel! Take your work over to the counter. Shauna, get on your chair and finish up." Watching with satisfaction as his orders were followed, Hank returned to his recliner. Following the rules was not news in his house; for that, he turned back to his newspaper.

A short while later, Hank glanced at his watch and cleared his throat. "Children," he announced. "It's 7:00. Your mother and I have dinner out this evening. I'd like to check your work now before I leave." He looked around the room. "Brianna."

Eight-year-old Brianna hesitantly approached her father, her week's spelling list in hand. By the time he quizzed her on her fourth word, it was obvious she hadn't studied the list. Hank removed his glasses and looked his daughter in the eye. "It is Thursday, Brianna. Your test is tomorrow. You have not studied your words, as you are expected to. If I do not see a 100 percent on this test tomorrow, you can forget about attending your friend's birthday festivities on Sunday." Brianna's eyes filled with tears, which had no apparent effect on Hank. "Do you understand me?"

"Yes, Daddy," she answered.

"Upstairs and get ready for bed. *Now.*"

Brianna trudged up the stairs, wondering how she was suppose to get a 100 percent when he was sending her up to bed instead of back to the table to study, but she knew better than to even ask. Her eleven-year-old brother was the next to be summoned. As he was making his way from the kitchen, the phone rang again. Shauna stood up. "Sit!" her father barked—and she did, with a heavy thump. Lucky for her, Hank couldn't see the murderous look on her face as she listened to her friend's second cheerful message. Shauna picked up her pen and furiously raced through her homework.

"OK, now . . . Ben. Show me the progress you're making on your homework packet." But a nervous-looking Ben approached his father holding only a dreaded red slip. Hank's brows lowered. "Another lapse in behavior? This is not acceptable." He held out his hand, into which Ben reluctantly placed the paper outlining today's infraction. Hank provided the required parent's signature, but Ben knew it came at a price, which was swiftly exacted as the address began. Hank's face was stern. "This is the third red slip you've brought home, and all three have to do with that brat, Jon, that you've been spending all your time with. Well, no more. I forbid you to play with him. There will be no after-school socializing. No weekend sleep-overs. And I will talk to your teacher tomorrow morning about moving your seat away from his." Hank gave Ben a severe look. "Do you understand?"

"Yes, Dad," Ben answered. During the remainder of his audience with his father, Ben's responses were short and crisp. Homework packet reviewed, he was sent upstairs with a harsh reminder that Jon was no longer an acceptable friend, and that he was not to spend any time with the boy.

Next was Rachel's turn. Hank was intent on reviewing her progress on her George Washington report but was annoyed with the messy stack of notes she handed him. "This doesn't look very organized, Rachel."

"Well, Dad, there's just so much information," Rachel shrugged. "I don't know what to write."

"Rachel, you are in sixth grade now. You need to buckle down and focus. No one is going to stand at your side and help you do your schoolwork. You need to sit down with these notes, concentrate, and make some sense out of them. I'll look over your progress on Saturday."

Thirty minutes later, Hank went upstairs to check that all four children were in their pajamas, washed, and reading quietly in their rooms. Satisfied that all was well, he stopped in Shauna's room for some last-minute oldest-child-baby-sitter rules before leaving with his wife to meet their friends for dinner.

As he settled behind the wheel, he looked over at his wife, and with a confident smile commented, "You're always telling me I'm too tough on the children. Well, my approach is obviously working. I think they're turning out to be perfect kids."

The Hidden Message

"I demand that you obey me, and obey me you will . . ."

Ahhh, but here's the rest of the story . . .

Perfect Kids, Part 2

Four sets of eyes were glued to the window, watching the parents drive off. Then, things began to happen.

Brianna looked over at the brightly colored package she had so carefully wrapped for Kristine's birthday party. With squinted eyes and furrowed brow, she thought, I'm going to the party on Sunday—and *nobody's* gonna stop me. She went to the closet and selected her outfit for the next day: jeans . . . and her green long-sleeve shirt. After laying her clothes out, she strode over to her desk with a look of determination in her eyes. With her black pen, she proceeded to copy her list of spelling words—onto the skin of her arm, which her long-sleeve top would cover discreetly until she needed a little help with her test.

As for Rachel, she gathered up her paperwork on George Washington and slunk downstairs to the computer. She called up her favorite term paper website and searched for reports on George Washington. Cool—plenty to choose from, she thought with a relieved smile. She picked sections she liked and printed out several pages of notes. Deciding that she might as well finish since she was already at the computer, she also printed out two final reports; she'd decide which parts to copy after her Saturday meeting with her father.

Ben quickly donned his sweatshirt and sweatpants over the top of his pajamas. He grabbed his jacket, then peeked into Shauna's room and announced, "I'm going to Jon's. I set my watch. I'll be back before *he* is . . ."

Shauna was on the phone but managed to answer, "Yeah, whatever." She closed the door behind Ben and giggled into the phone. "OK, Chad. You can come over. I'll leave my window open just in case you have to escape like last time . . ." Adolescent giggles filled the spaces in their conversation.

The Rest *of the Hidden Message*

" . . . but since I always tell you what to do and when, and since I've *not* taught you how to make your own decisions, or encouraged you to think for yourselves, or helped you develop self-discipline, I would be shocked to know what's going on behind my back."

Think About It

Parents who control their children with an autocratic style—one that shouts loud and clear, "My way or the highway!"—are often lulled into thinking that their chosen method of parenting is admirably functional. They often have the perception that their kids are perfect—which, of course, they are, as long as the parent is in the same room.

The truth, however, is not so rosy. Children who behave out of fear, children who behave only to prevent a parent's enraged outburst, do not develop the inner discipline that will serve them when they are away from the procurer of their obedience.

Many other side effects also derive from this style of parenting. Children raised in this kind of environment can learn to resent all authority figures. They come to see authority, rules, and laws as stifling and unfair.

These children also may have an inability to express their thoughts and feelings. They learn to cower under a cloak of compliance and to suffer quietly in their own ways.

Most notably, children who learn to obey without question do not learn how to critically evaluate options and make good decisions. When away from their parental authority figure—who, when present, does all the work of decision making—they search out a strong-willed peer to give them guidance. And sometimes they choose the wrong peer. Sometimes they choose the wrong crowd.

Certain defensive behaviors arise, as demonstrated in this story. If provoked enough, children learn ways to circumvent rules that they feel are unfair but at the same time still manage to appease the parent. They do this by becoming deceitful, defiant, and sneaky. The silent rebellion that occurs behind such a parent's back can devastate a child's future.

And at the heart of the situation, a dictatorial stance can erode the parent-child bond and prevent progressive, honest communication. If you were his child, could you see *yourself* having a loving heart-to-heart with Hank? Or do you see yourself eager to reach the age of majority and have the privilege of moving out of the house, and away from Hank, as fast as your legs can carry you?

No job is more important than raising your children, and exceedingly authoritative parents know this as much as other parents. The problem is not with the intention but with the delivery. They try too hard and fail to trust the innate good in their children, fearing that, without rigid guidelines, the children won't grow into decent, hardworking human beings.

Changes You Can Make

Maintain the control that you've already achieved—but temper it with new and different approaches that transform you into a more *benevolent* leader. The first step? Begin to see your children as thinking people who are in the process of learning inner discipline. Your job, then, is to present them with values and morals and encourage internalization of these qualities. This goes beyond making a command and ensuring that it's carried out. It means helping your children learn the reasoning behind the instruction. It means changing your primary job description from autocrat to mentor. It means changing your ultimate parenting goal from your children's daily obedience to their lifelong success. It means teaching them to understand the short- and long-term implications of behaving in the ways that you prescribe. And when they don't, sometimes it means allowing them to fail, and to make mistakes from which they will learn important life lessons.

Two-way communication is vital to having your children hear and accept your teachings. A more open presentation allows children to ask questions and participate—somewhat—in making everyday decisions. This will encourage them to evaluate their choices and become independent thinkers.

In addition, as children mature and gain more life experience, we need to increase the opportunities they have to make their own decisions. By treating fifteen-year-old Shauna and eight-year-old Brianna in nearly the same way, Hank is not allowing Shauna to grow up and assume control over her life, while in the same vein, he is expecting too much of his eight-year-old.

Children and parents both benefit from a balanced style of parenting that promotes obedience and, at the same time, nurtures independent thinking. It's a process that sends our children down the path to adulthood with strong backbones and healthy consciences, and allows us to trust that they can make good life decisions—even when we're not in the same room with them.

Hey, Guys, I'm Working in Here!

Ken is sitting at the kitchen table, immersed in his least favorite task—filling out tax forms. He's surrounded by checkbooks, calculator, piles of paperwork, and his favorite cup filled with coffee. His nine-year-old twins, Katie and Andy, are happily playing a game close by in the family room. All is quiet on this Saturday morning— at least until two high-pitched giggling fits break the silence.

Ken peers over his glasses at the source of the merriment. "Hey, guys, I'm *working* in here." The room settles into quiet again, but not for long. Game pieces suddenly find lives of their own, their rambunctious activities narrated by two young voices. Not even glancing their way, Ken grumbles, "You guys are being awfully noisy." The pieces continue their action in a whisper, and Ken again knuckles down to his work.

Not five minutes later, the game pieces engage in a mock battle that ends in a crescendo. Ken expresses his exasperation in two words: "Katie! Andy!" He drums his fingers on the work sheet and mumbles, "Why don't these kids ever listen to me?" He begins, once again, to wade through the endless tax forms. Just as the instructions start to make sense, his energetic young ones, now bored by their fantasy play, begin a mock battle of their own, complete with unbridled war cries and appropriate evasion strategies. The whooping flies around the room with the galloping kids.

Ken's daily patience reserve has been depleted—and to signal the event, he slams his pencil on the table, scrapes back his chair, and marches into the family room. With a bright red face, bulging eyes, and veins protruding from his neck, he bellows, "Katherine Nicole! Andrew Shawn! I have had *enough*! I need *quiet* to work! Either *be quiet* or *go outside* and play!"

The kids murmur, "Sorry, Daddy," as they shuffle out of the room and relocate to the swing set in the backyard.

Ken walks back to the table, his hands nervously combing back his hair, his breath labored. He's wondering why it always has to end this way.

The Hidden Message

"You don't have to listen to me until I get angry."

Think About It

Children are remarkably perceptive. They can tell when a parent means what he says—and when he doesn't. They learn to read the signs that tell them *when* they must obey. Sadly, with many parents, Ken included, this comes only at the point of anger. Ken's children have learned that they don't have to pay much attention to him until his face is bright red, his volume is turned to "extra loud," and he uses their middle names.

In addition to meaning business only when he's angry, poor Ken unwittingly has fallen into a common parenting trap set by unclear requests, confusing utterances, and half-baked pleas. His statements, while transparent to himself, lack distinct meaning for his children. For example, when he first announces, "Hey, guys, I'm working in here," a reasonable response could be, "Good for you, Dad; gotta get those taxes done." His next overture, "You guys are being awfully noisy," could conceivably be answered with, "You bet, and we're having a blast, too!" He follows these missives with a proclamation as clear as mud: "Katie! Andy!"—to which they could respond, "That's us!"

Not until he's angry does he actually use good parenting skills! (It's too bad that they are masked by his outlandish show of anger.) What does he do right? First, by getting up from his seat and walking over to his children, he finally breaks free of that disastrous imitation of discipline: yelling from two rooms away. Once he has the kids' complete attention, he actually makes a specific statement of his problem: "I need quiet to work!" He then gives them an explicit choice, one that clearly tells them what he expects: "Either *be quiet* or *go outside* and play!" Ahhh. Now they have specific instructions to follow. Now all Ken needs to do is learn to use these skills before his anger kicks in, then he'll find that his children listen to him without his needing to raise his voice.

Changes You Can Make

To prevent your having to resort to anger to get your children's attention, make the effort to use good parenting skills. Unless telepathy runs in the family, you can safely assume that your child can't read your mind. So, all those cryptic lines like "I'm working in here" won't help your child understand what you want. Instead, make a conscious effort to use specific statements that define what you want your child to do. The more definitive the statement, the better your child can understand your needs—and the more likely he will be to respond appropriately.

Eliminate wishy-washy utterances such as "It would be nice if you . . ." and "Don't you think you should . . ." Banish vagaries that require any guesswork from your child's perspective. Instead, think before you speak, and say exactly what you mean.

Keep in mind that these beautifully clear requests lose much in the process if they are shouted or mumbled from two rooms away. To be sure that your child hears you and pays complete attention, make the extra effort to go to your child, or call him to come to you. When you are eyeball-to-eyeball, you will have no doubt that your directive is being heard—and your child will have no excuse for ignoring you. Aside from that, yelling from another room is a rude habit that you, in your effort to raise polite children, would be wise to avoid.

Your clarity ensures that your child has all the information he needs to make a choice, but, alas, that doesn't guarantee that he'll do as you've asked. What if he makes the wrong choice and continues to misbehave? Well, that's another chapter, actually a whole 'nother book! (For specific suggestions, read my other books: *Perfect Parenting: The Dictionary of 1,000 Parenting Tips* and *Kid Cooperation: How to Stop Yelling, Nagging, and Pleading and Get Kids to Cooperate.*)

Index

About the Author

Parenting educator Elizabeth Pantley is the president of Better Beginnings, Inc., a family resource and education company. Ms. Pantley frequently speaks to parents in schools, hospitals, and parent groups, and her presentations are received with enthusiasm and praise. She is a regular radio show guest and is often quoted as a parenting expert in magazines such as *Parents, Parenting, Working Mother, Woman's Day, McCalls, Good Housekeeping,* and *Redbook* and on more than eighty parent-directed websites. She publishes a newsletter, *Parent Tips,* that is distributed in schools nationwide and is the author of two previous parenting books: *Perfect Parenting: The Dictionary of 1,000 Parenting Tips* and *Kid Cooperation: How to Stop Yelling, Nagging, and Pleading and Get Kids to Cooperate.* She and her husband, Robert, live in Washington state with their four children, Grandma, and assorted family pets. She is active in her children's school and sports activities and serves on the school PTA board of directors.

For More Information

To obtain a free catalog of parenting books, videos, audiotapes, newsletters, and lecture services available by Elizabeth Pantley, or to contact the author:

Write to the author at:
> 5720—127th Avenue NE
> Kirkland, WA 98033-8741

E-mail the author at:
> elizabeth@pantley.com or elizabethpantley@seanet.com

Call the toll-free order line:
> (800) 422-5820

Fax your request:
> (425) 828-4833

Visit the website:
> www.pantley.com/elizabeth

Search the internet for acticles by Elizabeth Pantley